THE NATIONAL ALLIANCE TO END HOMELESSNESS

WHAT YOU CAN DO TO HELP THE HOMELESS

THOMAS L. KENYON WITH JUSTINE BLAU

PRODUCED BY THE PHILIP LIEF GROUP

A FIRESIDE BOOK
PUBLISHED BY SIMON & SCHUSTER
NEW YORK   LONDON   TORONTO   SYDNEY   TOKYO   SINGAPORE

SIMON & SCHUSTER/FIRESIDE
Simon & Schuster Building
Rockefeller Center
1230 Avenue of the Americas
New York, New York 10020

Designed by Bonni Leon
Manufactured in the United States of America

1   3   5   7   9   10   8   6   4   2
1   3   5   7   9   10   8   6   4   2   pbk.

Library of Congress Cataloging in Publication Data
Kenyon, Thomas L.
What you can do to help the homeless: creative and effective contribution
that individuals, families, and businesses can make/Thomas L. Kenyon
with Justine Blau.
p.   cm.
At head of title: The National Alliance to End Homelessness.
"A Fireside book."
Includes bibliographical references
1. Homeless persons—Services for—United States.   2. Voluntarism—
United States.   3. Social service—United States—Citizen
participation.   I. Blau, Justine.   II. National Alliance to End
Homelessness.   III. Title.
HV4505.K38   1991
362.5'57'0973—dc20   91-7852
CIP
ISBN 0-671-74123-3
0-671-73734-1 pbk.

Special thanks to Constance Jones for suggesting the original idea for this book.

Thanks to the following for their assistance with this publication: Nan Roman, Michael Mayer, Jeff Klein, Sister Mary Scullion, Doug Lasdon, Philip Lief, and Julia Banks.

And above all we are indebted to Kara Leverte, whose direction energized this project at every stage.

CONTENTS

Introduction: You Can Do Something about Homelessness   9

You Can Understand Homelessness   11

You Can Treat Homeless People with Understanding   15

You Can Tutor Homeless Kids   17

You Can Recycle Necessities for Resettled Households   22

You Can Provide Child Care for the Homeless   26

You Can Register the Homeless to Vote   30

You Can Get Your Church or Club Involved   33

You Can Help Prevent Homelessness   38

You Can Teach Homeless Adults to Read   42

You Can Bring Joy to Homeless Children   45

You Can Write to Your State and Federal Representatives   49

You Can Get Your School or University Involved   52

You Can Help Provide Employment Counseling   57

You Can Give Runaway and Abandoned Teens Your Help   59

You Can Teach Your Children about the Homeless   62

You Can Provide Health Care as a Health Professional   64

You Can Get Your Business Involved   68

You Can Give Special Help to Homeless Substance Abusers   70

You Can Help Supply Permanent Homes for the Homeless   72

You Can Provide Legal Aid as a Lawyer   75

You Can Employ the Homeless   78

You Can Open Doors to the Mentally Ill   81

You Can Organize a Food or Clothing Drive   85

You Can Volunteer at a Shelter   88

You Can Lend a Hand to Homeless People with AIDS 92

You Can Know How to Respond to Panhandlers 94

You Can Give Special Help to Battered Homeless Women 97

You Can Raise Funds to Help the Homeless 102

You Can Volunteer at a Soup Kitchen 104

You Can Get Involved in Home Sharing 107

You Can Restore Life's Simple Pleasures to the Homeless 111

You Can Start a Food Recycling Program 113

List of Major Organizations that Help the Homeless 117

Bibliography 124

INTRODUCTION

YOU CAN DO SOMETHING
ABOUT HOMELESSNESS

Homelessness is one of the most serious social ills facing America today. The National Alliance to End Homelessness estimates that on any given night, over 300,000 men, women, and children live on the streets of the nation's cities, under bridges in the nation's suburbs, and in makeshift camps in the nation's rural areas. The homeless lack the food, housing, clothing, medical care, and educational opportunities most of us take for granted.

Virtually every American has witnessed homelessness in his or her community, and everyone shares a sense of despair and powerlessness in the face of this seemingly unstoppable scourge. Shamed, angered, and saddened by the sight of street people, we agonize, "What can an ordinary individual like me do about homelessness?"

In fact, you have many options. Whether you can commit a few minutes of your time or a few afternoons, the following chapters will present, clearly and simply, numerous ways you *can* ease the plight of the homeless and help make homelessness a thing of the past.

Remember, every successful program profiled in this book was started by a person who cared enough to take action—a person like you.

YOU CAN

UNDERSTAND HOMELESSNESS

At some time or other when you passed homeless people on the street or saw them on TV, you may have thought to yourself, "Why don't they get a job? Why don't they just take themselves in hand, do some honest work, save their money, and in no time they won't be homeless anymore?"

In fact, a growing number of *working* people are homeless. But the shortage of affordable housing in this country is so acute that many people in low-paying jobs—the cashiers in the fast-food restaurants, the stockboys in the department stores, the clerks in the supermarkets—cannot afford the cost of housing. Ironically, the poorest people pay the largest portion of their income for rent. A recent study showed that 63 percent of low-income renters spend more than 50 percent of their income on housing.

Misconceptions about homeless people are common, such as the ideas that many homeless people "want to live that way," and that the majority of them are mentally ill. In fact, the homeless population is a very diverse group. They include unaccompanied youths (4 percent), veterans (approximately 35 percent), people with chronic mental problems (approximately 25 percent), and people with substance abuse problems (approximately 25 percent). Families with children make up almost one third of the homeless population, and in some cities—such as Portland, Philadelphia, and New York—they represent the majority of the homeless.

The only things all homeless people have in common are that they do not have a place do live, and they are poor.

Here are some facts that dispel the myths about homelessness:

▸ Most homeless people are only homeless for a short while —but they may move in and out of homelessness periodically.

▸ Families with children are a fast-growing group among the homeless.

▸ The vast majority of the homeless, including those who are mentally ill, would prefer to have a home.

▸ The explosion of homelessness has surpassed the ability of local governments and charities to deal with the problem. All sectors of society must now play a role in solving it.

The factors that have contributed to the homelessness crisis include:

Loss of affordable housing. Gentrification, abandonment, and demolition have reduced the stock of affordable housing. Because of changes in the tax code, very little of this housing is being replaced.

Deinstitutionalization. In the 1950s state mental hospitals housed more than 550,000 patients. Today that number is fewer than 150,000, leaving a significant number of the mentally ill with no place to live but the streets.

Changes in family structure. There is an increasing number of single-parent households (which means one parent is carrying the burden of trying to take care of the children as well as work to support them). With diminished resources and support, a lost job, illness, or eviction can catapult a family into homelessness.

Cutbacks in federal housing and support programs. Aid to Families with Dependent Children, food stamps, and disability insurance income have not kept pace with the rising cost of living. Federal housing programs were cut some 70 percent in the 1980s.

Growing poverty. As many as 32 million Americans now live below the poverty line. More and more of these poor people just can't find a place to live.

The Homelessness Information Exchange reports in their book *Helping the Homeless in Your Community* that America need not—indeed should not—accept homelessness as a fact of modern life: "While some government programs should be curtailed or eliminated in the face of budget deficits, giving people a place to sleep at night and food to survive are not "luxury items" in a decent society. The United States, as the world's richest democracy, can surely provide its citizens with the basic requirements for physical survival."

Ultimately, what will help the homeless is more affordable housing. The current supply of low-income housing needs to be expanded by 5.5 million units if this nation expects to meet the needs of everyone who lacks adequate housing.

Elliot Liebow, author of *Tally's Corner* notes, "Surely homeless children who are moved into decent housing are less likely to become parents of homeless children than children who grow up homeless. Surely the person who is mentally ill or an alcoholic or an addict and has a place of his own is more likely to stand still long enough to profit from a program of treatment than someone living in shelters and on the street."

Along with housing, the homeless need services to help them cope, including:

▸ Day care and education programs for children
▸ Job training and employment assistance
▸ Alcoholism and substance abuse treatment
▸ Individual, family, and other counseling
▸ Psychological or psychiatric counseling and treatment
▸ Help in enrolling in benefit programs such as food stamps
▸ Education on nutrition and food buying and preparation.

Many of these services can only be provided by trained professionals, but there are countless other ways to offer assistance to the homeless—options open to ordinary people with a few minutes or a few dollars to spare. The simple measures described in this book can be an important first step in stopping the cycle of homelessness that afflicts our country. Try just one, and find out how easy it is to help—and how good it makes you feel. It's up to you.

The homeless need your support if they are to someday lead lives of stability and dignity.

● What You Can Do

1 Talk to your child and family about homelessness—its causes and its impact.

2 Speak out through letters to the editor or other means when the problems of homelessness are misrepresented in the media or by public figures.

3 Subscribe to newsletters, read articles, and watch or listen to specials on housing and homelessness to stay current on the issue.

YOU CAN

TREAT HOMELESS PEOPLE
WITH UNDERSTANDING

The minimum wage of $3.80/hour yields an income 20 percent below the poverty line for a family of three.
—Center for Budget & Policy Priorities

For many homeless people it requires a great deal of effort to take the necessary steps to get back on their feet. In the same way, homelessness around the country reached crisis proportions before most Americans became roused to action.

But no matter what level of political awareness each of us has, we're all capable of showing understanding to homeless people at the most basic level. Make eye contact with the homeless you meet on the street. Don't be afraid to smile and say hello to street people rather than walking by as if they weren't there. Acknowledging their humanity is one small, easy, yet extremely important way of helping the homeless.

Or maybe you're ready to get acquainted with a homeless person in your neighborhood—perhaps the same person you've been avoiding for months or years. As you get to know a street person, you will come to realize that the homeless are just like the rest of us. This understanding will benefit you tremendously, as well as bolstering your homeless acquaintance's self-image. The time may even come when you can help him or her to hook up with a social service agency and get back on the road to a stable life.

Understand that homeless people want the same things you do—sometimes they want to talk, sometimes they'd rather be private. If you become friendly with someone who's homeless, don't probe or push; just be an understanding friend.

IF YOU SEE A HOMELESS PERSON IN MEDICAL DISTRESS

As you would do for anyone having a medical crisis, call 911.

When you call 911 you should be prepared to give the following information:

▸ Where the person is
▸ What the person in distress looks like
▸ What the problem is.

Try to stay on the scene after calling 911 so you can provide support, if possible, or tell medical personnel what has happened.

IF YOU SEE SOMEONE HARASSING A HOMELESS PERSON

Again, call 911, just as you would want a bystander to do if you were being harassed. Ask other bystanders for help, but don't endanger yourself. Ask police to refer the person to a shelter or social service agency.

YOU CAN

TUTOR HOMELESS KIDS

Young people with weak reading and math skills are four times as likely to be dependent on public assistance as those with strong basic skills and eight times as likely to have children out of wedlock.
> —Lisbeth B. Shorr with Daniel Shorr, *Within Our Reach*

There are an estimated 222,000 homeless school-age children in the United States, and of that number, 67,000 do not attend school regularly.
> —*Homewords,* March 1990, Homelessness Information Exchange

Going to school presents special challenges to homeless kids. Because they're so mobile it's difficult to keep track of their school records, which makes it tough to register them in new districts as they move from shelter to shelter. Even those who do manage to register attend school irregularly. They may have no way to get to school, they may be too hungry or too sick to go, or they may have nothing to wear. Just as often, family crises make school a low priority. When they do make it to class, hungry, depressed, and anxious kids can't concentrate, which means they have trouble learning. And school gets even harder for homeless students if other children make fun of them for being different.

Whether they attend school or not, homeless kids often need special educational help. More and more often they are getting the attention they need, thanks to both volunteers and professionals. People who work with homeless students have discovered that one-on-one tutoring can give these kids the extra boost that makes all the difference.

In 1987, twenty-eight states received $50,000 or less in federal funding to assure homeless children and youth equal access to public education. The other twenty-two states received an average of $145,000.

Pam Selden is director of the Children's Center at Martha's Table, a community service center in Washington, D.C., where a successful tutoring program has been in place for two years. The Children's Center is in a neighborhood with serious drug problems, and there are several shelters nearby. Fifty percent of the children in the tutoring program are homeless. Currently thirty children are enrolled, and Selden hopes to expand to help sixty children this year.

"We try to provide support systems, not just tutoring," Selden notes. "We try to provide clothing and school supplies for both groups of children—homeless and neighborhood children—so that they can go to school and feel confident about the way they look. We also provide food for them. We're a soup kitchen, so we have access to quantities of donated food. We give the children an afternoon snack and a nutritious dinner before they're tutored."

Selden describes how the program works. "We are fortunate enough to have received a grant from the Ford Motor Company, which we used to hire a master tutor. He's in charge of helping our volunteer tutors. We have approximately thirty to forty volunteer tutors from all walks of life —high school students, professional people—and they come in the evenings and make a commitment to tutor their child once or twice a week. We ask them to make a three-month commitment at a time. This is very important because we have children who cry when their tutor doesn't show up."

The program's volunteers reap tremendous rewards from their work. Selden recalls one student's breakthrough.

"One of our students is Joey, an eleven-year-old who didn't

see any sense in going to school, and he really felt poorly about himself. He really improved in his schoolwork—his grades have improved. There was a question about whether he could advance to junior high school, and he made it. He now feels very self-confident and he insists on the other children calling him Dr. Joey."

There are several things that Selden thinks have contributed to the success of the tutoring program. "We have workshops for our tutors. We try to support them by speaking to them often, troubleshooting for them, providing materials for them. Sometimes our children don't have homework, so we have devised a system where every child has a folder with math and reading and spelling at her level. When a child doesn't have homework, the tutor and child can still get right to work."

Much of the program's effectiveness comes from the support and encouragement children receive there. "We have dinner, and that's a wonderful time for the tutor to talk with the child," Selden notes.

"We also have a little reward system. At the end of the evening the children receive a pencil or some candy or a school notebook. The children feel that they do a good job—and everyone gets the same thing, whether they've had a good tutoring session or not. We tell our tutors that it's especially important to accept the children where they are. We have some children who are working below grade level and some who are working far above grade level."

The program, Selden explains, extends beyond the traditional school year. "We had an awards ceremony at the end of our school year, where each child received a trophy in recognition of their participation. And we tutored throughout the summer. We think it gave the children an extra edge and built or maintained skills that might have been lost over the summer.

"Another reason the program works is because of the support system. We try to use caring, consistent tutors who genuinely love the children. And we try to encourage the parents to work as our partners.

"We work for the common goal of helping the children be all that they can be."

● **What You Can Do**

1 If tutoring programs for homeless children already exist in your local school or shelter, volunteer to help. Call homelessness groups and other charitable organizations to find out what kinds of programs they are operating, and ask how you can get involved. You'll typically spend one afternoon or evening a week or a few hours each weekend working with kids in a structured environment. Look for a program that provides tutor training and has a qualified staff liaison to give you back-up support.

2 Arrange for your church, club, business, or school to contribute services or supplies to a tutoring program. Your club or church can donate space or refreshments; your business can offer paper, pencils, art supplies, or the use of a van; your school can supply tutors, classrooms, and rides. Any group can raise funds to support a tutoring program, through bake sales, raffles, or car washes. Perhaps your group will want to make tutoring homeless kids part of its regular schedule of activities.

3 Work with your club, church, or other group to set up a tutoring program in cooperation with a public school. Contact school officials and ask for their help in designing a program. Tell them how many kids you will work with. Once plans have been made, you'll need the help of one qualified teacher to oversee the program, generally recruited from the staff of the school you're working with. The school, a shelter, a church, or your group can provide a space in which to conduct the program, and businesses will be eager to donate your basic supplies and transportation for the kids. On an ongoing basis you should keep in close contact with the school so you can keep track of the results of your work.

● **Contact**
National Association of State Coordinators for the Education of Homeless Children and Youth
1701 N. Congress Avenue
Austin, TX 78758
(512) 463-9067
Contact: Joe Johnson

Monitors the activities of tutoring programs for homeless children nationwide. Offers assistance to groups wishing to start tutoring programs in their communities.

YOU CAN

RECYCLE NECESSITIES FOR RESETTLED HOUSEHOLDS

What we throw away can feed and clothe everyone in need.

—Eileen Rogers, Orlando
Coalition for the Homeless

It seems like it will last forever, but the ordeal of being homeless does end for most people, and their dream of moving into a stable home comes true. Many resettled families, however, find themselves sleeping, sitting, and eating on the floor. They have to start from scratch to find basic furniture, like beds, tables and chairs, and other household necessities. Completely furnishing a house would be a strain for any family, but it's especially hard for the recently homeless. They usually have just enough money to pay the rent, utility, and food bills.

You can assist the homeless making the transition back to a stable life by donating furniture and appliance items.

Annette Allyn Day, a typesetter in Atlanta, Georgia, collects donations of household goods and, operating out of her home, distributes them to formerly homeless people who are just getting resettled into housing.

Day assembles the small items into what she calls "home kits."

"People are referred from all over Atlanta and different agencies to get this home kit," says Day. "It's a box of rawbones basics that people can carry away in their arms. It's very immediate. They can call and make an appointment to pick up a home kit on Saturday. The basic home kit is worth about $100."

A home kit includes items needed for the kitchen, bedroom, and bathroom. Typical items in a home kit include:

For the kitchen: a can opener, eating utensils, a pot and a frying pan, maybe a hot plate (if there is no stove), a few plates, bowls, and glasses.

For the bedroom: some sheets, a pillow, a blanket, maybe a clock radio.

For the bathroom: towels, wash cloths, toilet paper, soap, shampoo, toothbrushes.

Other important items that might be included in a home kit:

Lamps
Books
Curtains
Throw rugs

For children:

Clean toys in good repair
Stuffed animals and squeeze toys
Building blocks
Trucks

Day gives out about seven home kits a week. "We get our donations from private individuals (although it would be wonderful if we had hundreds of pots and pans that a big cookware company might donate). But we're not so much interested in great quantities as we are in really talking with someone and pulling together things they really need.

"This whole thing boils down to friendships, getting to know the person. The greater successes come when there has been a long period of acquaintance, meeting their basic needs for survival, such as shoes, socks when their socks are wet, having a shirt or a pair of trousers—building trust. Many homeless people do not trust people; they have good reason."

In addition to distributing the home kits, Day also collects and distributes used furniture to newly resettled people, operating out of a big basement donated by her church. A volunteer helps her by collecting donated furniture in his pickup truck every weekend. About five formerly homeless people come by every Saturday to get beds, tables, and other furniture for their new homes.

"There was an elderly gentleman who came to work when we had a system whereby people worked at the basement to earn credits to get furniture," Day recalled. "He worked so diligently to save his credits until he had lots of them. Then when he picked things, the things he chose were so nice. Big paintings, nice chairs, an avocado green rug. I imagine his apartment was real pretty in a handsome, sturdy sort of way.

"Many people choose pretty things before they choose useful things, because beauty inside little apartments is so important," Day notes. "In neighborhoods where there's no grace and no shrubs and no flowers and trees, it's a relief to have beauty.

"I give plants away. Homeless people like plants, and they're expensive to buy."

Day advises people not to think that they need to have a giant organization in place in order to distribute household necessities to the homeless. "A person does not have to have a lot of money to do this, because I certainly did not go into this with a lot of money. But it touched my heart and I got busy and I did something.

"I love it so much I can't think of facing a day when I'm not doing this," Day asserts.

• What You Can Do

1 Go through your home and find any household items in good condition that you no longer need or use. (Remember to set aside usable discards *whenever* you're cleaning out your closets or the attic.) Call the Salvation Army or look through the Yellow Pages for local organizations that accept donations for the homeless, and arrange to drop off your donations or have them picked up. By passing your unneeded things on to resettled families instead of to the dump, you'll help others, get a significant tax deduction, and benefit the environment, too.

Your donation of the following used items can help displaced people settle into new homes:

Furniture, such as beds, dressers, tables, sofas, chairs, desks, cribs, wardrobes, bookshelves

Appliances, such as lamps, clocks, vacuum cleaners, televisions, radios, telephones, dishwashers, refrigerators, washer/dryers

Household essentials, such as dishes, glassware, flatware, pots and pans, kitchen utensils, brooms, mops, buckets, tools, rugs, sheets, towels, curtains, windowshades

Gas stoves and cooking devices such as toaster ovens, microwaves, and hot plates (since many apartments do not provide stoves).

2 Donate your time and skills to a furniture collection drive. If you own a van or truck you can pick up and deliver items; if you're handy around the house you can fix, refinish, or clean donations. And anyone can help keep track of inventory. Lending a hand can be fun: you'll meet new people and really feel good about yourself.

3 Start a furniture collection program of your own at your church, school, or club. Get in touch with a group that resettles homeless families and coordinate your efforts with theirs. Members who drive vans, pickups, or station wagons can provide transportation; donations can be stored in a spare classroom, basement, or meeting space. In order to attract donations, you can publicize your program through fliers and newspaper advertising. Ask donors to bring small items in, but arrange to pick up large items from them. Before storing donated items, inspect, sort, and record them, and clean or repair anything that needs attention. In conjunction with your partner agency, set up one day a week when resettled families can come look over the donations and choose what they need. After that, all you need do is deliver the items to their new address.

● **Contact**
The Sponsorship Program for Homeless People
P.O. Box 54555
Atlanta, GA 30308-0555
(404) 892-6404
Contact: Annette Allyn Day

Contact your local homeless coalition, homeless service program, or Salvation Army for information about what's needed.

YOU CAN

PROVIDE CHILD CARE FOR THE HOMELESS

Children are the poorest group in society, with more than one in five living in a household whose income is below the poverty level.

—House Select Committee on Children

Despite medical advances, the infant mortality rate in the United States is worse than in some third world countries.

—Children's Defense Fund

When families with young children become homeless, it is the children who suffer most. Homeless parents are often under too much stress to be able to give their children the attention and care they need. Homeless children are often poorly nourished and sleep deprived. Sometimes they have behavior problems because of an unstable or difficult family life.

Volunteers at day-care centers for the homeless can give children the thing they crave most—individual attention. Playing games with children, reading to them, encouraging them, listening to them, singing songs—all these wonderful activities can allow a homeless child to blossom and feel good again.

Day-care centers also need volunteers to perform chores such as shopping and cooking, or they can help provide transportation to and from the center for the children.

Another way you can help is to get your school, church, or other group together to provide a one-time volunteer effort at a day-care center for homeless children. You might decorate a playroom, build outdoor play equipment, or organize a Christmas drive to bring presents to the children.

Among low-income families with children, average household income fell 14 percent from 1979 to 1987.
In 1987, 48 percent of black children lived below the poverty line.

Our House, Inc., is a day shelter in Decatur, Georgia, that provides a safe, nurturing environment for thirty homeless preschool-age children each day. While their children are at Our House, parents are free to look for work or begin working, and to search for permanent housing. Without such free day care, parents with small children find it almost impossible to work and save money so they can move out of shelters and into permanent housing. Our House depends on a total of thirty volunteers, each of whom works a day or two per week.

Our House provides the following services:

The preschool program at Our House provides quality day care five days a week from 7:00 A.M. to 6:00 P.M. for homeless children under six years old. The children are given breakfast, lunch, and a snack each day.

The school-age program helps place older children in afterschool and summer programs.

Health care is provided for parents and children at a local clinic and hospital. And a nurse and health advocate visit Our House every week.

A family resource program helps the parents find work or job training, and helps them find housing and get the benefits they're entitled to, such as food stamps, veterans' benefits, and Aid to Families with Dependent Children.

Vee Huie is a grandmother and a boardmember of her church in Atlanta. She's been volunteering at Our House for a year now, for three hours a week.

"I was at a stage in life where I had time to give. I really wanted to be involved directly with the children and see how they felt to be homeless."

Huie recalls her shock at what she saw on her first day at the center. "The first time I went I was really overwhelmed by some of the aggressiveness and the hostility—understanding it but at the same time being overwhelmed by it. Particularly one child was one of the most hostile children I have ever seen. He always seemed to be in conflict with other children, yanking away their toys from out of their hands. I've raised four sons and I have grandchildren, so I've had experience with children, but this was almost scary to me."

Nonetheless, Huie returned to Our House and watched as the caring atmosphere began to make a difference. "In the matter of six weeks' time, I saw startling changes in this one child. And I think this was mainly because the whole thrust of Our House is for the individual child to develop a sense of self-worth."

The center has also had a positive impact on Huie's life. "Now all my grandchildren are far away, and I think I miss having my own. So I spend my time in the baby room—I like rocking the babies. There are three little girls in there now, triplets." The volunteers do all kinds of things with the children. "We go out on the playground. I had four children in four swings today, pushing them. We read stories, change diapers, help feed them.

"One man built a playhouse on the grounds. Others have helped with the yard work. There's a lady who comes in once a week with a guitar and her own little girl and plays songs. She sits on the floor and the children sing with her."

As rewarding as the work is, volunteers still face problems. "You can be discouraged by the problem of homelessness. I would come home sometimes a bit overwhelmed, when you saw all those children and realized they had no place to go, no space to call their own," Huie reflects.

"If you think of the economy and how difficult it is now, you can easily become discouraged. But we have to start somewhere," she asserts. "If we are going to change society, children have to have some sense of their self-worth."

Huie notes that the requirements for being a successful day-care volunteer are simple. "If you're going to volunteer with homeless children, you really have to have a love for children. There are such rewards," she continues. "The little boy who frightened me my first day here—he told me one day, 'I hate you.' I hadn't done anything. But in the period of time that he was with us he went from saying 'I hate you' to saying 'I love you,' which was a huge benefit to me. It made me feel like a million dollars. And I came home and told my husband, 'Barry's changed. He likes me now.' "

● **What You Can Do**
1 Contact local shelters, transitional housing programs, or the United Way, Salvation Army, or other local service agencies to find out about volunteer opportunities at area programs for homeless children.
2 Find out if there is adequate day care for homeless children in your community. If not, mobilize your church or service club to do something to fill the gap.
3 Donate books and toys—new and used—to programs for homeless children. Collect them at home and from your friends and neighbors.
4 Do you have a hobby or talent you can share with children? Tell stories, hold a painting class, or give lessons on a musical instrument to homeless children.

● **Contact**
The Children's Defense Fund
122 C Street, NW
Suite 400
Washington, DC 20001
(202) 628-8787

Provides advocacy on behalf of poor, minority, or handicapped children. Call or write for a free publications list.

YOU CAN

REGISTER THE HOMELESS
TO VOTE

The statistic about voting that's most often quoted is that only 50.1 percent of all Americans voted in the 1988 presidential election. But of the people who were registered to vote 86.2 percent turned out. When people are registered, they vote. *And there are 70 million unregistered Americans.*

> —Louise Altman, One
> Hundred Percent Vote (a
> project of The Human Serve
> Campaign)

Disenfranchised and often isolated, homeless people usually don't know what their rights are. One of these rights is the right to vote, even if they don't have a permanent address.

The act of voting can help make a person feel that he or she is a member of a community. And by voting, the hundreds of thousands of homeless people in this country can become a very potent force in the struggle to secure adequate housing and services for all Americans.

Will Daniel, director of Homeless Voter '90, has registered 3,000 homeless people to vote in New York City in the last two years. "Obviously you need to feed and clothe and shelter people," he says. "But to me attacking poverty means more than that. If you want long-term solutions, you have to bring the people who have the most at stake into the process. And anyone can become political—everyone is interested in what happens in their communities. But for various reasons people come to feel alienated and left out."

Daniel outlines his group's concerns. "We've been doing an opinion survey, and we asked, 'What is the worst thing about being homeless?' And the persistent answer is depersonalization. 'People treat me like I'm a peace of meat.' 'People treat me like I'm not there.' 'People think the homeless are hopeless.' 'People think the homeless have no minds.'

"Part of our theory is that voting makes you a citizen," Daniel explains. "It reinvests you in the community. And that has a very personal benefit on the individual."

But the effects of voter registration for the homeless go much further. "The other important thing," Daniel notes, "is that homeless people have real political power. Homeless people tend to be concentrated, so they can have a disproportionate impact in local elections. There are shelters with a thousand men. My project works extensively with a soup kitchen that serves a thousand lunches a day. And those places become communities. People are by necessity associating in public and they're likely to feel a community sense. That makes it easier to organize them and motivate them to vote. And obviously they have a lot of compelling needs in common—housing, job training, more public assistance."

Daniel speaks enthusiastically about his goals. "Most candidates are saying to themselves, 'Homeless people don't vote.' But there are voters out there who care about what happens to homeless people. So candidates can't at least appear insensitive to homeless people. I'm hoping that some of them will take a position and maybe some action that will be good for homeless people."

Daniel became interested in registering the homeless almost by accident. "A friend called me and said she wanted to start up a volunteer project. I originally pictured it as a couple of hours a week, but I liked it more than that. So I do it full time, thirty to sixty hours a week.

"It's easy and it's fun," Daniel says. "What I've found with my volunteers is there is initially a personal hurdle to be gotten over between white, educated, middle-class people and homeless people. And some fear. And even a little revulsion. And once you get over that and see these people as human beings, it's rewarding. You make friends. So the personal hump is the thing."

● **What You Can Do**

1 Get in touch with existing voter registration efforts and political candidates who are mounting registration drives. Ask them to arrange to register homeless people at some of the following spots:

▶ Shelters (day and night)
▶ Transitional housing programs
▶ Soup kitchens
▶ Appropriate parks and other places where homeless people congregate.

2 Call local programs for the homeless and ask if you, or a group you are working with, can distribute voter registration materials (usually obtainable from a board of elections) and help people register. If they'd rather not have you set up on the premises, maybe you could just drop off the materials.

3 You can obtain a resource book on voter registration from

U.S. Catholic Conference
Office of Domestic Social Development
1312 Massachusetts Avenue, NW
Washington, DC 20009

● **Contact**

For information about how to register the homeless in your community, call or write to:

Homeless Voter '90
149 West 10th Street
New York, NY 10014
(212) 989-1002
Contact: Will Daniel, Director

YOU CAN

GET YOUR CHURCH OR
CLUB INVOLVED

During the 1980s, homelessness grew at a rate of about 25 percent a year. Homelessness now affects every region and every type of community—downtowns, suburbs, and rural areas.
—Homelessness Information
Exchange

Churches, temples, and civic clubs around the country provide immeasurable assistance to homeless people. Many churches and temples serve free meals on a regular basis and offer a variety of services to the needy. Many congregations support permanent housing programs. Civic clubs regularly organize events to raise money for charity. If you would like to mobilize your congregation or club to help the homeless, here are some project ideas, gathered from religious and civic groups nationwide.

Begin by choosing *one* issue relating to homelessness that your parish or club can concentrate on. Make sure you interview as many parishioners or club members as possible to get a consensus on which issue to make a priority.

Contact local programs to see what their needs are.

Publicize, through your bulletin board or newsletter, a list of local service projects for which congregation or club members could serve as volunteers for a few hours a week or month. Include soup kitchens, shelters, transitional and permanent housing programs, and anti-poverty groups.

Suggest that your parish donate a percentage of your

weekly collection to a project—operated by the church or by an outside group—to help the homeless.

Organize a working support group for the unemployed in your parish or club. See if you can link their skills with the needs of potential employers within the area. Put together a job bank, referral service, and résumé-writing program.

Start a food co-op or food-buying club within the parish or club. (A food co-op is a group, usually staffed by volunteers, that buys food in bulk—at a discount—and sells it to members at low prices.) Make sure that you invite low-income people in your community to join the co-op and help operate it. Contact your local food stamp office to learn about how low-income people can use food stamps to buy food from the co-op.

Develop a plan for your parish or club to winterize the homes of needy families and the elderly of the parish next fall. Make an effort to involve youth in all aspects of the project, including procuring materials and performing manual labor.

Volunteer as a parish, temple, or club to prepare and serve a meal at a local soup kitchen on a regular basis. A good way to implement this plan is to involve many different organizations—the youth group, the choir, etc.—within your parish, and assign responsibility for each meal to a different group on a rotating basis.

See if there is a building or space in your parish or club to house programs for low-income or unemployed people. If space can be found, develop plans and collect funds to convert the space for its new purpose.

Organize a letter-writing campaign to your congresspeople, calling for more funding to build low-income housing and to finance programs that will help end homelessness. Educate your fellow congregation or club members about the issues of homelessness by distributing literature and newspaper articles and by talking with them.

Invite political candidates to speak at your parish, temple, or club before the next election. Be sure to invite members of other churches and community organizations to participate in the forum. Question the candidates on what steps they are taking to end homelessness.

St. Steven's Episcopal Church in Washington, DC, provides free showers to the homeless. Frank Chiancone, the parish administrator, feels that his church is filling "a serious need" of homeless people in the area.

"We get between twenty and thirty-five men every morning," says Chiancone. "And it's not only homeless people. We get a lot of individuals who live in boardinghouses where maybe there are no shower facilities. We have people who come up from the shelter because it's too crowded there in the morning.

"We have three stall showers. There's a sink. A lot of people drop in to shave.

"One of the biggest problems of the homeless is to be presentable when they go for a job interview. We will give them a clean white shirt for that."

Do you have problems with people taking too long in the shower? "We have a sign up that says don't take more than ten minutes, but we really don't enforce it. Some of them come in on their way to work or to a job interview and they get annoyed if people take a long time.

"One thing that has plagued us is that towels walk away. We're constantly begging parishioners to donate towels. We don't have a staff person to monitor it. We just put a whole box of towels and soap and shampoo out. A lot of them take a towel and after they've showered and changed they come back and take a dry towel. We lose a couple of towels every day."

What suggestions can you offer churches that would like to set up bathing facilities? "We have found that the hotels are good about donating soap. Hotels collect used soap from the rooms, and we go collect a box of it every two months, so that's not a problem. But hotels use their old towels—they cut them up for dust rags. So we're dependent on parishioners. So if you're going to set this up, have a system where you hand them one towel. Once the towels are wet, they don't take them.

"Another serious need they have is to clean their clothing. Many of them come with a bag of clean clothes but many others take a shower and have to put really dirty clothes back on. We don't have a facility to launder their clothing. If we had the space . . . it's a constant request."

● **What You Can Do**

1 Have your group take responsibility for creating one unit of affordable housing. You could raise money to pay for rehabilitating a house or apartment. You could purchase a property or get one donated and fix it up. The house could then be operated by your group or turned over to an area nonprofit organization. If every congregation in the nation did this, there would be virtually no shortage of affordable housing.

2 Have your congregation or club take responsibility for the children in a program for the homeless—providing field trips, tutoring, or mentoring.

3 Have your organization or club take responsibility for housing one homeless family or individual. Work with a local shelter or transitional program to help find and, if necessary, subsidize an apartment or house. Help out with follow-up support.

Project Home Again, a program of World Vision, helps churches do just that. The local Project Home Again site coordinator links a homeless family with a caring church. The church commits to pay first and last months' rent, security deposit, and an additional month's rent, and helps the family settle in. A trained ministry team from the church helps the family with other needs like transportation, furniture, etc. The site coordinator and ministry team do follow-up for a year. World Vision trains the site coordinator.

4 Contact a local homeless program and offer to do follow-up for re-housed homeless families. Keep in touch with them, provide support, and communicate their needs back to the program counselors.

● **Contact**
Project Home Again
U.S. Ministries Dept.
World Vision, Inc.
919 W. Huntington Drive
Monrovia, CA 91016
(818) 357-7979
Contact: Jana Webb

YOU CAN

HELP PREVENT HOMELESSNESS

A recent survey by the Partnership for the Homeless found a widespread increase in "hidden homeless" families—those doubled up in overcrowded and/or substandard housing, at risk of ending up on the street at any moment. A recession could plummet large numbers of them into homelessness.

Hardly ever does a landlord *want* to evict tenants because of back rent owed. It's a cold, nasty business to uproot people from their home. Sometimes it's heartrending. And on the practical side, once a tenant is gone, it's almost impossible to collect back rent. Furthermore, going through the process of a court eviction costs time and money. So more and more landlords are cooperating with agencies that run eviction prevention programs.

Over the last five years the Red Cross in Warren, Ohio, has helped 600 clients stay in their homes through their eviction prevention program. "Any church or agency or community could set up a like program because it's rather simple in nature," says William Mottice, executive director of the Trumbull County Chapter of the Red Cross. "It's a selective program. You have to look at those who you can really help. It's not a bottomless pit. There are some people you can't help. If you just pay a month's rent to buy thirty days of living space and don't solve any other problems, the cycle will just start all over again. You can best help those who can help themselves."

Mottice continues, "We look at those people who have the

possibility of returning to work or getting entitlements so they can continue paying their rent.

"If you select a person who is down and out but they're down and out because they were laid off, then you can see that in a few months this person has a chance to be self-supporting.

"People on the verge of homelessness. That's where we should home in. Because if you can be preventive, you can do it cheaper and better."

Jeannine Taylor is the director of Emergency Services for the Red Cross in Warren. She recounts the following story, one among hundreds, of a family saved from homelessness by the eviction prevention program.

"A woman came to my office last January with five small children. She works at Arby's where she clears $358 a month. Her rent is $250 a month. She was behind in her rent because she didn't have medical insurance and she had to buy medicine for her children. She was unable to get caught up and she received an eviction notice from her landlord.

"We talked with her and suggested she apply for Aid to Families with Dependent Children, which would also get her food stamps and medical coverage. She refused to go because she was afraid her husband would find her and beat her. She would be made to tell his name and where he was so that the Department of Human Services could track him down to make him pay support. The last time she did that he tracked *her* down and beat her and raped her and got her pregnant again. She didn't want to take the chance of him finding out where she and the children were.

"So she filled out an application and we gave a $250 check to her landlord that brought her up to date. And she continued on all right.

"She seemed like a very caring mother. Her only goal in life was to work to raise her children and keep them in a decent home. She was the tiniest little thing. She said if she has to work two or three jobs she'd do it.

"She knows that should she need more help she can come

back. We try and leave all the clients with the feeling that they can return should they need some assistance. If we can't help them, we'll find somebody who will."

● What You Can Do

1 If you're a landlord and you're thinking of evicting somebody because they're not paying their rent, see if you can work with a social service agency to find a way to prevent that eviction. The agency may have resources to pay the rent, or they may have a tenant/landlord mediation program that could help establish a payment schedule for your tenant and provide them with the support they need to keep to that schedule.

2 If you know of someone who is about to be displaced or evicted, help them get in touch with a local service agency that may be able to provide them with the funds to prevent their eviction.

3 Volunteer to work with a follow-up program. Sometimes people who have been homeless don't have the equipment or housekeeping skills that make people good tenants. If people are moving into homes after being homeless, they're not likely to have a lawn mower or vacuum cleaner. You can help support them by recycling equipment such as lawn mowers, vacuum cleaners, and washing machines to help stabilize them in their homes. Alternatively you can volunteer to help them mow their lawns or clean their houses every week.

● Contacts

The American Red Cross
625-661 Mahoning Avenue, NW
Warren, OH 44482
(216) 392-2551
Contact: Jeannine Taylor,
Director of Emergency Services

For information on assisting an eviction prevention program or if you are interested in setting one up.

Emergency Food & Shelter National Board Program
601 N. Fairfax Street
Suite 225
Alexandria, VA 22314
(703) 683-1166

The board is the national coordinator for the distribution of federal emergency food and shelter funds, which can be used for prevention programs.

YOU CAN

TEACH HOMELESS ADULTS
TO READ

As many as 27,000,000 Americans are functionally illiterate. Another 35,000,000 read below survival level.
—Street News, September 1990

On average, an illiterate adult earns 42 percent less than a high school graduate.
—Laubach Literacy Action

People who lack basic reading skills almost invariably face a bleak future. They are handicapped in performing even the simple tasks of daily life because they can't read newspapers, street signs, maps, or directions for operating appliances or for cooking food. They can't get a driver's license and they're unable to fill out forms to apply for jobs. Living with such limitations, illiterate people have a very slim chance of holding jobs and maintaining their independence.

Learning to read is of paramount importance to the illiterate homeless. It gives them a fighting chance to break the cycle of homelessness.

The high school drop-out rate in the United States is 27 percent. In Japan the rate is 5 percent and in the Soviet Union it is 2 percent.

Seventy-five percent of unemployed adults have reading or writing difficulties.
—Jonathan Kozol, Illiterate America

The members of the Orlando Coalition for the Homeless are thrilled with the success of their adult literacy program.

"A lot of the homeless have been in special classes and labeled as limited learners," says Eileen Rogers, director of the program. "We've had a number of people find out that they do have academic strengths.

"I ran it as a pilot project for a year and a half with my own money," Rogers says of the literacy program. "I had given up my job and I used to walk around downtown, inviting people to come to class.

"We taught creative writing, introduction to art, psychology, and video as literature. Every Wednesday we saw a movie with a particular theme and the students would write about it in creative writing and draw pictures about it. Finally we got a grant from the McKinney Homeless Assistance Program, as well as other federal, and state money."

The program, which has been running three and a half years, now employs three teachers, two clerks, and ten volunteers.

"We had a student, Nick, who had been in Vietnam, and who was turned off and sour. He used to do a routine about how the whole experience of Vietnam had ruined him. He was on the street about three or four years. We confronted him about his behavior . . . and he started to go to school with us. He stopped being involved in his own misery and became committed to keeping a job. He trained as a welder —and that earned him enough money to go to college. Last I heard, he's going to the community college, working, and able to pay for one or two classes at a time.

"The bottom line was: we cared."

Rogers offers this advice to people who want to tutor the homeless, "Let them decide what it is they want to read. It may be too high for them but work with them. If they want to read *Playboy,* romance novels, the Bible, whatever."

● What You Can Do

1 Call homelessness groups and other charitable organizations to find out if they are operating a literacy program, and ask how you can get involved.

2 Arrange for your church, club, business, or school to contribute services or supplies to a literacy program. Your club or church can donate space or transportation; your business can offer paper, pencils, refreshments, or the use of a van; your school can supply tutors. Any group can raise funds to support a literacy program, through bake sales, raffles, or car washes. Perhaps your group will want to make volunteering for a literacy program part of its regular schedule of activities.

3 Once plans have been made, you'll need the help of at least one qualified teacher to oversee the program. A shelter or a church can provide a space in which to conduct the program.

● Contacts

Literacy Volunteers of America
5795 Widewaters Parkway
Syracuse, NY 13214-1846
(315) 445-8000

Push Literacy Action Now (PLAN)
1332 G Street, SE
Washington, DC 20003
(202) 547-8903

YOU CAN

BRING JOY TO HOMELESS CHILDREN

What agency do we create, what budget do we allocate, that will supply the missing 'parental affection' and restore to the child consistent discipline by a stable and loving family?
— James Q. Wilson, Harvard
Professor of Government

Both common sense and research tell us that as family stress, regardless of its source, increases, the capacity for nurturing decreases, and the likelihood of abuse and neglect increases.
— Lisbeth B. Shorr with Daniel
Schorr, *Within Our Reach*

One aspect of homelessness that is most distressing is that children make up approximately one quarter of the homeless population. Homeless children often have sleeping and eating disorders and suffer from listlessness hyperactivity, aggressiveness, depression, anxiety, and more medical problems than other poor children.

Growing up amid stress, instability, and poverty, homeless children miss out on many of the pleasures of childhood. The support network that other children take for granted—attention from grandparents, uncles and aunts, neighbors, participation in church activities, Cub Scouts and Brownies, friends in the neighborhood—is simply missing.

But, like any other children, when they are treated with tender loving care they respond beautifully.

What can one do to give these kids a break?

"Just take them out of the environment they're in and show them what other environments are like," suggests John Turcott, who works with the Partnership for the Homeless in New York. "In the environment they're in, the most successful people—according to their perception of success—are drug dealers.

"The main thing is to give them some attention," Turcott says simply.

Ironically, foster care families receive more financial assistance than natural parents to care for the same child.
—Homelessness Information Exchange

● What You Can Do

Here are some things you can do to bring joy to homeless children. It's usually best to go through an established social service agency.

1 Get your club or church—or just some friends—together and see if you can arrange to take homeless children from a local family shelter on field trips one Saturday or Sunday a month. You can take them to such things as:

▶ Baseball or basketball games
▶ The zoo
▶ Children's theater matinees
▶ The movies
▶ Museums
▶ Bowling
▶ Special events like fireworks or parades
▶ Ice skating
▶ The aquarium.

2 Coach homeless kids in baseball, soccer, volleyball, or other sports on weekends.
3 Collect a load of children's books from your friends, ac-

quaintances, co-workers, and your own attic, and donate
them to your local family shelter.
4 Volunteer to pay for a homeless child to go to summer
camp. Make sure to contribute enough to buy the clothes and
equipment they'll need.
5 Become a Big Brother or Big Sister and request to be as-
signed to a homeless child.

Remember that it's important to honor any commitment
you make to the children—whether it's a one-time trip or a
regular monthly outing. Homeless children have had their
faith and trust shaken. What you're trying to do is show them
that you care and that you respect them enough to fulfill your
promises to them.

"It's like feeding birds," comments Havelock Hewes, a
teacher who worked at the Children's Storefront School in
Harlem, New York City. "You have to keep feeding them all
winter because they come to rely on it. If you don't feed them
they'll die.

"We had volunteers who came to the Storefront, spent time
with the kids, took them to ball games, then stopped coming.
Our kids got depressed and angry. Volunteers need to main-
tain commitment."

Maintaining your connection to homeless children is easier
if you make your program as accessible to them as possible.
Provide transportation to and from events. Plan events requiring parents' signatures—such as summer camp—far in
advance so you have plenty of time to secure permission for
children to participate.

CHRISTMAS

Christmas is a magic time for children. No matter how
squalid the circumstances, how jaded the child, come Christmas all children dare to hope that they will find coziness,
presents, good cheer, loving parents—and a secure home.
You may not be able to bring a child a home or an intact
family, but you can work on the rest of the wish list.

Invite everyone at your office, church, or other group to donate a Christmas-wrapped toy for a homeless child and bring the presents to family shelters.

Arrange for your club or office or other group to hold a holiday party for homeless children.

When you help kids feel good, their joy is contagious—it makes you feel good.

While Christmas is a rewarding time to help, many programs are inundated with help then and receive little at other times of the year. Think about having Christmas in July—and spreading the cheer to another season.

● Contacts
Big Brothers-Big Sisters
511 North Broad Street
Philadelphia, PA 19123
(215) 625-2455

Look in the phone book for your local chapter or contact the national office in Philadelphia.

Save the Children Federation
54 Wilton Road
P.O. Box 950
Westport, CT 06881
(203) 226-7272

Or contact your local programs for the homeless.

YOU CAN

WRITE TO YOUR STATE AND
FEDERAL REPRESENTATIVES

*The number of housing units renting for less than $300
per month—the amount a family can afford on a $12,000
per year salary if they pay one-third of their income for
rent—declined by over 1 million units between 1974 and
1983.*

> —Checklist for Success,
> National Alliance to End
> Homelessness

In the early 1980s, when homelessness in this country
reached a crisis level unseen since the Great Depression, advocates for the homeless learned it costs less to keep a family
in its home than it does to provide emergency services. Short-
term emergency assistance, while vital, is not going to stop
homelessness. If we don't want to raise a generation of children in homelessness, we must address its deep rooted
causes. These include cutbacks in federal housing programs,
the conversion of low-income housing units to luxury housing,
lack of facilities providing mental health care, changes in the
family structure, and substance abuse.

By writing to your state and local representatives, you can
let them know that you think providing affordable housing
and adequate services for everyone is a top priority.

● What You Can Do

1. Keep up to date on the issue by following it in the local
media and getting on the mailing lists of local and state homeless and housing coalitions. Local programs for the homeless

may publish newsletters you can subscribe to. Or you can subscribe to newsletters put out by national groups (see List of Major Organizations that Help the Homeless, p.117), including:

> National Alliance to End Homelessness
> National Coalition for the Homeless
> Homelessness Information Exchange
> National Low Income Housing Coalition
> Emergency Food and Shelter National Board
> Interagency Council on the Homeless

2 Look at government activity on homelessness in your community. Here are some of the things to evaluate:

▸ Is there adequate shelter to meet local need?
▸ Is there adequate transitional housing?
▸ Are adequate efforts being made to move people into permanent housing?
▸ Are there policies to preserve existing affordable housing?
▸ Are homeless children adequately provided for?

Plus, keep informed about other issues of concern to you, such as health care and education. If you are dissatisfied with performance in any of these areas, contact the appropriate local official. Your voice *will* make a difference.

If you want to write letters to public officials, your local public library has their addresses. Letters to your members of Congress can be addressed as follows:

> (for your Senator)
> The Honorable _____
> United States Senate
> Washington, DC 20510

> (for your Congressman)
> The Honorable _____
> U.S. House of Representatives
> Washington, DC 20515

You can call your Senators and Congressmen through the Capitol Switchboard at (202) 224-3121.

● **Contact**
The National Coalition for the Homeless has a twenty-four-hour hotline to convey information about what individuals can do to lobby Congress on behalf of homeless persons. A recorded message with the latest information on pending legislative issues can be heard by calling (202) 265-2506.

YOU CAN

GET YOUR SCHOOL OR
UNIVERSITY INVOLVED

Volunteers working with the National Student Campaign Against Hunger and Homelessness raised $200,000 in the spring of 1990 by participating in a national work-a-thon.

—National Commission on
Excellence in Education

College students are in a unique position to help the homeless. In the university environment, students are in constant contact with other students—at the dining hall, in the dorms, at the student union, in classrooms, around campus—and so they have an ongoing opportunity to rally to get involved in helping the homeless.

Since students are at a point in life where they're especially interested in learning new things, they're often open to participating in worthwhile projects—especially if these projects are fun. Sometimes students can get academic credit for helping the homeless if they become interns or volunteers at approved facilities.

In the spring of 1990, four students at Georgetown University Law School decided they wanted to help the poor and homeless in their community. By fall they had organized a spectacular volunteer program and mobilized many of their first-year classmates to join them.

It all began when the four students started talking about how difficult it was to find a volunteer project that fit into their busy schedules. They felt the law school should have an organization that informed students about social service agencies in the city that needed volunteers. So the students,

Michele Lavin, Julia Parsons, Valerie Schultz, and Gretchen Butler started it themselves.

"We sat down and discussed what we wanted in this entity yet to be born," remembers Butler. "We talked it out, called it Georgetown Outreach, set long-term and short-term goals, and made a presentation to the dean.

"The school has been incredibly supportive. They gave us an office. We got office equipment donated by a law firm. They gave us a desk, chairs, computer. They were superb."

The students put in a lot of time to get the program off the ground quickly. "Over the summer one person got academic credit to work on the project," Butler says. "The other three of us put in tons of time.

"Our main focus is to facilitate individual volunteering through the community," Butler explains. "We have notebooks with listings of various agencies in the city. We sorted the agencies into categories—homelessness, children, literacy/tutoring, cultural groups, elderly, legal related. Many are cross-listed."

Butler describes how the program works: "A student walks into the office and says, 'I'm interested in working with homeless children.' We refer them to these books where they can look through the listings. Each agency has a page with location, contact name, brief description of the agency itself, its purposes, the agency's need for volunteers, estimated time commitment, and flexibility—that's a big issue for law students. If someone is interested at first glance, we have more information in our files."

The program's focus is simple. "Our whole thing," Butler says, "is to make it as easy as possible for students and staff and faculty to get involved in volunteering in the community. Everything we aim for is ease of participation."

When school started in the fall, the students organized a volunteer kick-off day, involving 175 student volunteers, 75 homeless kids, and nine events. Some students took homeless children to a farm ("a lot of these kids have never seen cows and corn," notes Butler); others repaired an emergency shelter; some went to a teenage group home and helped the kids clean their rooms.

"Our goal is to have a big event and a smaller-scale event each semester," says Butler. "The response has been overwhelming. We're working with Good Shepherd Ministries to take kids on field trips on Saturdays. Seventy-five or eighty people signed up for that. That's really awesome. That's an unbelievable response—a lot of law students are hesitant about obligating themselves to anything."

Butler summarizes the benefits of the program. "You're working with students on a level different than law. You really get to know people better. It's sparking a community spirit in a law school that's the biggest in the country and historically has had a reputation of being large, corporate, and cold.

"I think that among students there's been a sense of working together and doing something constructive," she continues. "I'd like to emphasize our focus is not just for people who have an undying need to volunteer. They would do it anyway. We love those people, but our focus is to make volunteering part of education, so that people realize, 'Hey, I can be involved in the community on a greater level.' "

What helped the program work so well? Butler lists the things the four women did right: "We came up with a very, very organized plan. We approached the administration first thing. We told them, 'We want to do this for the school, but to do it we would like you to help us.' We had weekly meetings where we set long-term and short-term goals. We made sure communication between us was good. We made ourselves so visible on campus that you'd have to be a moron not to know who we are."

Based on her experiences, Butler has the following suggestions for other students who are starting programs for the homeless: "When you make mass mailings, follow-up is very key. Anytime you make a commitment to an agency or to anybody, make sure it's carried through. And if it can't be, make sure you let them know at the earliest possible moment.

"We stress to our volunteers, number one: quality, not quantity. It's better to say you'll be there one hour a week and be there, than to promise a lot of time and have to cancel. Because these people are counting on you."

● What You Can Do

1 Try to establish an internship program that gives credit for working with service organizations for the homeless.

2 Do an article or series of articles about homelessness in the student newspaper. Interview homeless people, service providers, and public officials, as well as students.

3 Organize students to help with data gathering in research projects involving the homeless. Contact your local homeless coalition to find out how you can help.

4 Talk to existing school organizations about the problem. Encourage them to get involved.

5 High school students with good reading or math skills can volunteer at a tutoring program for homeless children.

6 Organize a special dance to which students receive a reduced admission if they bring a clean blanket. The blankets can be distributed to homeless people on the street or donated to nearby shelters.

7 Conduct a free-throw basketball contest, with contestants paying a fee to participate. The money raised can be donated to an organization that helps the homeless. Or, establish an admission charge of two cans of food to the opening season basketball game and donate the food to a shelter.

8 Put on a carnival at school, with the proceeds going to a homeless shelter.

9 Elementary schools can adopt a family shelter and the children can donate their old toys, books, and clothes to the children at the shelter.

10 Conduct a food drive and bring donations to your local shelter or food pantry.

11 Students can collect donations of *summer* clothes. (Most shelters get plenty of winter clothes, but people forget that homeless people need summer clothes too.)

Georgetown Outreach
600 New Jersey Avenue, NW
Washington, DC 20001
(202) 662-9262
Contact: Tricia McHugh

● **Contacts**

The Georgetown Outreach program welcomes calls from people at other universities and colleges who are looking for assistance in setting up similar programs.

National Student Campaign Against Hunger and Homelessness
29 Temple Place
5th floor
Boston, MA 02111
(617) 292-4823

The National Student Campaign Against Hunger and Homelessness has a resource center in Boston, Massachusetts, which is available to anyone who is involved with the issues of homelessness and hunger. They'll give you information to help you organize a group on campus. They can also tell you about homeless advocacy organizations and facilities with internship programs that allow you to get academic credit for your volunteering experience.

YOU CAN

HELP PROVIDE
EMPLOYMENT COUNSELING

For anyone who wants to work, to be unemployed creates a world with no future, a world that quickly slips into despair. Work is for sustenance. It is also a critical step in turning a life of isolation into one of participation and actuality.

> —"Helping the Homeless Find Permanent Jobs," Jubilee Jobs, Inc.

Being unemployed can be crushing for anyone, but for homeless people, the obstacles to finding employment are staggering. It's the ordinary things—things that people in stable environments don't even need to consider—that deter homeless people from finding work. These include:

Not having an address to write down on an application form

Lack of a telephone where employers can reach applicants

The difficulty of maintaining good hygiene, grooming, and proper interview clothes

The cost of transportation to interviews, and to and from work until the first paycheck comes.

Even if a homeless person manages to get a job, he or she must make a mighty effort to adjust to working conditions, because the culture of the workplace may have become alien to the isolated, brutal world that homeless people live in.

Another problem homeless people face is lack of motivation. After perhaps months or years of dealing with bureaucracy, dependency, lack of dignity, perhaps battles with substance abuse and loneliness, they cannot easily face the prospect of a new job with enthusiasm.

● **What You Can Do**

1 You can volunteer to help a job counselor for the homeless by:

▸ Making a presentation to clients on what you or your company look for when you interview and hire.
▸ Taking part in role-play interviews.
▸ If you have access to a video camera, volunteering to tape role-play interviews. This can help clients improve their interview skills.

2 You can also:

▸ Donate appropriate clothes for interviews.
▸ Volunteer to help people with grooming for interviews.
▸ Volunteer to transport and/or accompany people to interviews.

● **Contact**

For a copy of the manual "Helping the Homeless Find Permanent Jobs," contact:

Jubilee Jobs, Inc.
2712 Ontario Road, NW
Washington, DC 20009
(202) 667-8970

The manual costs $5.

YOU CAN

GIVE RUNAWAY AND ABANDONED
TEENS YOUR HELP

*Every year about one million young people under
eighteen run away from home. About 6 percent remain
on the streets indefinitely and become "street kids."*
—Covenant House

One of the most exciting things about volunteering with
teenagers and young people at risk is that they're still so
impressionable. A caring person, offering understanding, ac-
ceptance, and guidance, can have a beneficial and lasting in-
fluence on young lives.

Teenagers who run away or who are homeless for other
reasons are often traumatized. Many of them have had the
bleakest family lives and have been physically, sexually, or
emotionally abused. They may be involved with drugs or
prostitution. Being a teenager is hard enough, but homeless
kids have a lot of additional problems to deal with. As a re-
sult, working with teenagers can be very demanding. But for
some people, the thrill and fulfillment of making a difference
in a young person's life is the best experience around.

Cookie Frankowitz of Fort Lauderdale, Florida, is a forty-
nine-year-old mother of two grown children. She's also a volunteer who works with at-risk teenagers at Covenant House,
an agency that specializes in assisting runaways and throwaways (children who have been forced out of their homes).

Once a week Frankowitz goes to Covenant House and takes
young people, eighteen to twenty-one years old, on a recrea-
tional outing. These young people are in a twenty-eight-day
addiction management program, trying to free themselves

from substance abuse. During this period, they're not allowed out of the building, except with a staff person or on a supervised outing with volunteers like Frankowitz.

"I take them bowling or to a park so the kids can play ball," Frankowitz says. "I can take from one to six kids. We sit and talk, or we can walk around, do a nature trail. Whatever is drug free. We're trying to get them back into society without using drugs.

"When I first started doing this I was nervous. I didn't know what was expected of me or what I expected of the kids. As it progressed, I've learned to accept them as they are. I go in there and I don't care what they have done. I can give them understanding, show them that I care. Hopefully they'll pick something up that they'll remember later on in life, that will help them have the courage to live without drugs. Some of these kids have not been able to get past the dysfunction of their families. They're using drugs to cope with life."

Frankowitz offers this suggestion to people who would like to volunteer to help at-risk teenagers: "Hang in there. They can be very manipulative and controlling. If you're willing as a volunteer to really understand these kids and accept them, you can grow along with them. You have to get past the point of taking things personally. I had one kid who said, 'I now have respect for you, because I can't manipulate you or control you anymore.' "

Frankowitz continues, "A lot of people say they want to do this, but they don't take that risk and go ahead and do it. I went down there and I found out it isn't a risk. I've learned to enjoy going down there."

Typical assignments for people working with at-risk teenagers include:

▸ Riding in an outreach van
▸ Working on hotline phones
▸ Tutoring
▸ Counseling
▸ Teaching parenting skills to teenage parents

- ▶ Working with kids just coming off the streets
- ▶ Recreation
- ▶ Sorting donated clothing, so kids coming off the streets can have fresh clothes
- ▶ Becoming a mentor to a young person.

Covenant House, one of the largest resources for runaway and at-risk young people, prescreens volunteers and gives them twenty hours of training. Volunteers are asked to commit to four hours a week for at least six months, or if they need a shorter time frame, to commit to 100 hours in all. The organization accepts volunteers from all walks of life.

"No experience is necessary," says Kevin Callahan, volunteer coordinator of the Fort Lauderdale Covenant House. "We concentrate on commitment."

● **What You Can Do**

Teenage runaways generally cannot stay in adult shelters, and few places have shelter space specifically for youngsters.

1 Find out if such space is adequate in your community. If not, write to your mayor and the media, and encourage them to investigate the problem.

2 If you know of youngsters who are in danger of leaving home or being forced out (throwaways), help them by finding out where they can get professional assistance.

3 Contact your local school to see if it has counseling for runaways. If not, encourage the school to develop special programs.

● **Contacts**

The National Runaway Hotline
(800) 231-6946

Covenant House
(800) 999-9999

Or contact your local shelter to see if they need volunteers to work with at-risk teenagers.

YOU CAN

TEACH YOUR CHILDREN ABOUT THE HOMELESS

If there is an implicit bias in the United States it is this: Families should be self-sufficient, and if they're not, they deserve to suffer.

—Dr. T. Berry Brazelton

Homeless people are often shunned or mistreated because others don't understand their problems or blame them for their predicament. If we are going to solve the problem of homelessness, we must begin with compassion and understanding. And what better place to start than with our children?

"It's so important for children to learn about caring and compassion," says Susan Baker, chairman of the Alliance. "We have to help our children understand, and not reject, people who seem different to them. And we should expose them early on to the importance of volunteerism and giving by being involved ourselves."

• What You Can Do

Here are some ways that parents can teach their children about homelessness—and even do something about it:

1 When your children reach the age of ten or twelve, you can volunteer as a family at a foodbank or shelter.

2 As a family you can help build or renovate homes for the poor through groups such as Habitat for Humanity and Christmas in April.

3 High school–age young people can be encouraged to volunteer at boys and girls clubs or to get involved in a tutoring program.

4 Suggest to your children's school administrators that they have a special lesson on homelessness.

5 Teach by example. Show that you care about and respect homeless people, and your child will, too.

"We have to teach compassion," stresses Baker. "If we don't expose children to the problems of the world and to other children like themselves, their own age, who come from different environments, they may not outgrow their childhood biases.

"It's the one way we as a nation are going to be able to break the cycle of poverty, by instilling in our young people a sense of compassion for those less fortunate than themselves. And until that happens, government leaders, local politicians, and businesspeople will not be moved to any type of constructive action."

YOU CAN

PROVIDE HEALTH CARE AS A
HEALTH PROFESSIONAL

It could happen to anybody. When you lose your health, you really feel helpless.
> —Carol Thompson, former
> homeless person

As homeless people are often exposed to the elements, poorly clothed and fed, and certainly under great stress from the exertion of trying to survive in unstable conditions and without resources, their health, both mental and physical, suffers. Health care professionals are in a unique position to lend them assistance.

Dr. Joshua Stillman works in the emergency room at Columbia Presbyterian Hospital in New York City. Many of the patients he treats are homeless, and treating them can be difficult.

"The first problem some caregivers face is fear," says Dr. Stillman. "Fear of contracting an illness like tuberculosis, or fear of an unpredictable patient. It's physically unpleasant to examine some street people. Doctors are not trained to deal with these problems in medical school.

"Besides the physical element is the fact that many of the homeless are psychologically troubled," Dr. Stillman continues. "That makes it hard to identify their true medical problems. And you know whatever you try to do for them isn't going to be easy for them to carry out once they leave the hospital. Most of the time there is no follow-up. They will not return. It is my assumption always that I will never see them again.

"Overall, the circumstances on the street are so adverse.

Medications they might have get lost or stolen. And they're sleeping in the rain or snow."

Dr. Stillman describes the medical conditions typically faced by homeless people: "The problems they come in with include pneumonia—that's life threatening because they don't come in until they're already very sick. Tuberculosis, which is endemic in shelters, is a major problem. There's a lot of skin infection; leg ulcers; scabies (a form of crabs); frequently they have seizures from either drugs or physical trauma; intoxication from various sources is frequent— there's a lot of drug abuse; AIDS is frequent; infections of the blood; complications of the effect of the drugs, as in the case of crack; extraordinary physical exertion and exhaustion, associated with muscle breakdown and kidney failure."

But health care professionals *can* make an impact. Dr. Stillman remarks, "An integral part of providing care is caring about who you're providing care for. Understanding more about the person frequently makes that possible, although it's not easy to get that information. They're just as frequently hostile to you.

"Frequently the life story that led to their situation is a tragic one and is very human. And connecting to them as a human being helps one take care of them better. But it's extremely hard not to become disenchanted and alienated from them. Homeless people complain frequently that they're treated like animals."

Health care professionals like Dr. Stillman treat the homeless as best they can, but as with poor people in general, there's no reliable system of health care.

"I really feel like society has to take care of them. If they were fed and clothed appropriately to their environment and had a home, all the medical issues would be simple. There probably are unemployed, dysfunctional people in every society—and somehow other societies take care of those people better.

"We need a social umbrella to take care of these guys. There are times I feel tough-minded. A lot of these people seem like they could work and it's their fault. It's not clear why one person can do and another person can't. So when I

say we need to keep alive the sympathy, I don't say that in the bleeding-heart sense. It's not only out of principle that you have to treat people as human beings. It's also a fact. These people just don't function the way we do in society. It's part of our own dignity to give them dignity."

● What You Can Do

Here are some ways health professionals can volunteer to help the homeless:

1 Encourage greater involvement of health professionals in homelessness. Working through the local American Medical Association is one way to do so.

2 Work with your Junior League, Chamber of Commerce, or other civic group to encourage other health care professionals to get involved in programs to help the homeless. Requests from these groups can be persuasive.

3 Contact your local Health Care for the Homeless project or other homeless service organization and volunteer.

4 Accompany outreach teams to the streets to diagnose seriously ill people and treat minor ailments.

5 Become an advocate for better health care for homeless people.

● Contact

If you would like to volunteer as a health professional, you can find ways by contacting:

National Association of Community Health Centers
1330 New Hampshire Avenue, NW
Suite 122
Washington, DC 20036
(202) 659-8008
Contact: Freda Mitchem

Freda Mitchem, who works for the National Association of Community Health Centers, suggests these ideas for how physicians and health professionals can help the homeless:

"Getting physicians' services in low-income areas is not easy," Mitchem notes. "Some physicians don't want to serve low-income communities because they don't like the reimbursement rates they get under Medicaid. They don't like the fact that some individuals don't have any medical insurance at all. In some instances they find it threatening or distasteful to serve low-income people. That general avoidance many people have is magnified when you're dealing with homeless people.

"Most physicians haven't been trained in community settings. It's really a different kind of health care, much more holistic, much more responsive to the community, and much more mission-driven than is private practice.

"The homeless health care issue in this country is part of the issue of lack of medical care and health insurance for the uninsured. Most homeless people are not medically insured, and most providers tend to shun homeless people.

"The best thing a physician could do is be an advocate for a national health insurance program or an insurance program for the uninsured. The point is, the homeless are the most disadvantaged, the most vulnerable, the most disorganized of the poor. They're so disadvantaged that they've even lost the roof over their heads. They have tremendous health problems, and the poorest of the poor don't have health insurance. They don't have any card that they can take anywhere to anybody to say, 'My leg hurts, can you help me out?' Charity is it.

"A doctor who is in private practice can work with the AMA or National Medical Association to ask them to incorporate in their legislative platform, which they present to Congress every year, full funding of the McKinney Homeless Health Care Program. We'd love to see the AMA do something to advocate full funding. We'd welcome that support. We'd love to see the mainstream professional health organizations play a more active role in advocating better congressional appropriations for this program.

"Health care for the indigent is a drop in the bucket in terms of the broad agenda of the AMA."

YOU CAN

GET YOUR BUSINESS INVOLVED

Of the $114.7 billion donated to charities by individuals, foundations, and corporations in 1989, corporate gifts comprised only 4.4 percent.
—Estimates from "Giving USA," an annual report of private sector contributions in 1990 by the American Association of Fundraising Council.

One of the most effective ways to help the homeless, and potentially one of the most fun, is to find ways to use resources at your place of business. Across the nation, the combined efforts of working people, with the financial backing of their businesses, have made an enormous difference in the lives of the homeless.

Some people can use the same skills that they work with every day to help the homeless. For instance, in Panama City, Florida, about eighteen members of the local homebuilders association organized a Saturday workday to repair the homes of needy people in the community.

But most businesses find alternative ways to help the homeless. For instance, a division of Manufacturers Hanover in New York decided to forgo their annual client party, instead donating what it would have cost to groups that help the homeless. Clients received a card explaining the change and telling them that the donation had been made in their name.

• What You Can Do

1 Whether your business is large or small, there are countless ways you can help.

▶ Haircutters at a beauty salon could arrange to go to a transitional housing program and cut hair.

▶ Lawyers can donate their time to advise clients if they have legal problems.

▶ Architecture and interior design firms could help renovate buildings and space to use for housing for the homeless.

2 Other ways to involve your business include:

▶ *Having your business adopt a shelter* or transitional housing program. Employees at your business might provide transportation to help clients find an apartment or a job; take responsibility for tutoring children; provide job training—or jobs—to some clients, and so on.

▶ *Organizing benefit performances* and donating the proceeds to a local program helping the homeless.

▶ *Conducting a food drive,* asking people to buy one nonperishable item, and donating the food to your local soup kitchen.

3 Here are some points to keep in mind:

▶ Make sure you hook up with an organization that has experience working with volunteers and has enough staff to help you carry out your program.

▶ It usually works out best if your business or group concentrates on one project, rather than taking on too many projects.

▶ Expect everything in a community service project to take longer and involve more obstacles than your usual work because you're doing something unfamiliar and relying on volunteers.

▶ To be effective, volunteers must be well trained, well scheduled, and well supervised.

● **Contact**
The National Alliance to End Homelessness
1518 K Street, NW
Suite 206
Washington, DC 20005
(202) 638-1526

The Alliance has a booklet on what corporations can do to help end homelessness.

YOU CAN

GIVE SPECIAL HELP TO
HOMELESS SUBSTANCE ABUSERS

A relationship built on trust and respect is the foundation for bringing about positive changes in another person's life.
> —*Working With Homeless People,* Columbia University Community Services

If you work with homeless people, you are likely to encounter problems with substance abuse, since as many as one fourth of homeless people are substance abusers. Drugs and alcohol can temporarily ease boredom and loneliness, or lift a person's spirits despite an unpleasant environment. It is understandable, then, that homeless people, living without creature comforts, stability, dignity, or sometimes even hope, often find drinking or taking drugs appealing. Getting high or drunk may be the only way they know of alleviating their pain and disappointment, regardless of the toll substance abuse ultimately takes on their health, family life, earning power, and self-respect.

Whether you volunteer at a soup kitchen or a transitional housing program, or ride around in an outreach van, you will come into contact with homeless substance abusers. In general, as a volunteer the best thing you can do for homeless substance abusers is to be supportive and offer information. If a substance abuser knows you respect him or her as a person, and if you avoid expressing disapproval or staging a confrontation, you may be able to offer valuable help to someone who needs it. When that time comes, be prepared with referral information about a community organization whose social worker can help get the person into a detox center. If you are working in a shelter or other facility where there are homeless substance abusers, here are some tips to keep in mind:

Make sure you clearly understand the program's policy regarding drugs and alcohol, and enforce it firmly and consistently.

Be supportive, but if a guest comes in high or inebriated, it is in everyone's best interest that you abide by the rules (even if that means having to ask him or her to leave). When in doubt about what to do, turn to the facility's staff.

You may be tempted to make an exception for someone you know particularly well, but doing so could do him or her more harm than good.

People who abuse alcohol and drugs generally have deepseated and complex problems. Sympathy, understanding, and information may not be enough to help them. Your efforts can leave them hostile and you frustrated. Make sure you are working as part of a team that includes experienced professionals.

● What You Can Do

1 Read up on the nature and symptoms of substance abuse.

2 Arrange for an authority in substance abuse or for a recovered addict or alcoholic to speak to your group of volunteers.

3 Advocate more local detox and drug abuse centers.

4 If you see someone on the street who is inebriated or otherwise out of control, particularly if they are in danger or are a danger to others, call 911. Try to keep them in sight until help arrives. It may be best not to interfere with them unless it is an emergency.

● Contact
The National Self-Help Clearinghouse
25 West 43rd Street
Room 620
New York, NY 10036
(212) 642-2944 (9:00 A.M. to 5:00 P.M.)

Provides referral services for people looking for self-help groups.

YOU CAN

HELP SUPPLY PERMANENT
HOMES FOR THE HOMELESS

*In New York and Boston there is less than a one per-
cent vacancy rate in low-income rental housing.*
—Homelessness Information
Exchange

*In 1985, 2.5 million persons were involuntarily displaced
from their homes, while 500,000 low-rent units are lost
each year.*
—National Housing Law
Project

Throughout the 1970s and 1980s, the stock of affordable
housing in the country dwindled as buildings were renovated
into luxury housing, converted to co-ops and condominiums,
or abandoned. In Boston, for example, rents skyrocketed by
a staggering 329 percent between 1970 and 1985. The equa-
tion is simple: when low-income housing is lost, poor people
are forced out onto the street.

Helping to actually *build* homes for people who need them
is one of the most satisfying jobs you can do. Ask former
president Jimmy Carter. He gives time every year to work
with Habitat for Humanity, helping to construct homes for
the needy.

This nonprofit, Christian organization was founded in 1976
by a minister, Millard Fuller, to construct homes for the
working poor. Headquartered in Americus, Georgia, Habitat
now has chapters worldwide and has built more than 3,000
houses for low-income families.

The families selected for the program don't have to put any money down, but they are required to help build their homes with "sweat equity." That means they must spent 300 to 500 hours working on their own or someone else's home.

"Habitat's solution to the housing problem is a hand up, not a handout," says Carter. "It seeks to break the cycle of poverty by working in partnership with needy families to construct new homes. In the process, we build dignity, self-confidence, and self-reliance."

Habitat builds simple but sturdy and affordable homes for less than $30,000, because most of the materials and labor are donated. The families are given interest-free loans to pay off their mortgages.

The idea of helping to build a house can sound intimidating, but if you can simply drive a nail, carry lumber, handle a paint brush—or even type—Habitat can use your help. The willingness to work hard is the main requirement.

The categories of volunteer work that Habitat needs include:

Construction skills: masonry, carpentry, dry sheet rock, painting, flooring

Office skills: secretarial, word processing, receptionist, accounting, bookkeeping

Journalism skills: writing and photography to put out Habitat's newsletter

Computer programming

Public relations and publishing skills: to raise funds and plan special events

In-kind donations and soliciting skills: to obtain building materials such as lumber, carpeting, plumbing supplies, tools, etc.

● **What You Can Do**

1 If you have low-cost apartments or rooms available for rent, list them with a local transitional housing program. Ask the transitional program to provide follow-up assistance to tenants who were formerly homeless.

2 Make a socially responsible investment in affordable housing. Contact your local community foundation or nonprofit housing developer to find out about the possibilities in your area. Or contact LISC or the Enterprise Foundation (see List of Major Organizations that Help the Homeless, p.117).

3 Make sure your bank is doing its part to create affordable housing. Banks are "graded" on whether they meet the credit needs of their communities, including those of low-income people and the homeless. These "grades" (Community Reinvestment Act [CRA] Reports) are increasingly available to the public. If your bank is not doing enough, encourage it with letters and/or meetings to invest in low-income housing.

4 If you are in the development or construction trades, work with local nonprofit organizations to develop low-cost housing.

● **Contact**

If you would like to volunteer to work with Habitat for Humanity, you can contact them at:

Habitat for Humanity
Habitat and Church Streets
Americus, GA 31709
(912) 924-6935

YOU CAN

PROVIDE LEGAL AID
AS A LAWYER

If you want to represent homeless people as a lawyer, you can't wait for them to come to your office. You have to go where they are.

—Doug Lasdon, founder of the
Legal Action Center for the
Homeless

Homeless people are usually overwhelmed by their situation and the troubles that have led them to be homeless. Because they have no cash or resources, their energy is consumed by the struggle of day-to-day living. Since they are so exhausted, both mentally and physically, the idea of rebuilding their lives—of securing permanent housing, job training, a job, drug rehabilitation—seems hopelessly out of reach.

This is where lawyers come in. Lawyers can help homeless people negotiate their way through the bureaucracy of social services, inform them of their rights to government assistance, and help them win back assistance if it has been illegally terminated or denied.

Doug Lasdon founded the Legal Action Center for the Homeless in New York City in 1984. Operating out of an office in the East Village, the group—comprised of lawyers, paid advocates (who work to locate assistance for the homeless), and volunteers—does several kinds of work for the homeless.

Legal clinics in soup kitchens. "The homeless generally don't know they have rights," says Lasdon. "They don't know where to go to vindicate themselves if they do know they

have rights. And if they get there, they'll probably have a
hard time getting someone to accept their case. So we've
brought the service to them where they are most comfortable
and where they can be heard.

*Law reform, class-action lawsuits, and other systemwide
advocacy.* "We sued the foster care system for improperly
discharging eighteen-year-olds, thousands of them every
year. We won a regulatory scheme that requires mandatory
pre-discharge training. Now you cannot be discharged unless
it's to an appropriate setting available for a year." (This
means that young people leaving the foster care system don't
end up homeless at eighteen.)

"We sued the grocery stores for violating the bottle bill by
refusing to let people redeem cans. We also sued the city for
splitting up married couples, requiring men to go to the men's
shelter and women to go to the women's shelter."

Issue research reports. These include a reference manual
to help social workers find permanent housing for their
clients, and a national study on service to youth after foster
care.

"Every day we have success. We bring twenty-five admin-
istrative hearings [lawsuits against the city, state, or federal
government to help a person get social benefits if they have
been terminated or denied] every month and win over 90
percent of them. We'll have a class-action suit that helps thousands of people. And every day, just by sitting down with
homeless people, we touch their lives and help them—just by
talking to them and listening and being there with them, as a
lawyer and as a person."

● **What You Can Do**
1 Donate your services directly to represent homeless people
through legal aid and other legal service organizations. This
could include representing people in housing court so they
don't become homeless. Or representing battered homeless
women in property settlements and custody disputes.
2 Help homeless people get government entitlements. Some-

times this is as simple as counseling them that *they are entitled to social services* even if they have no address and no identification. (This information can mean a world of difference to homeless people. It can lead to their getting cash benefits, disability benefits, food stamps, and Medicaid, all of which helps them to stabilize and get off the streets.)

3 Provide legal assistance to nonprofit organizations that help the homeless. That includes:

▶ Assisting in incorporation
▶ Assisting in finance development
▶ Assisting in contracting and housing development
▶ Assisting tenants' associations.

4 Try to get your law firm to provide pro bono assistance to a group or groups helping the homeless. Encourage your local bar association to get involved as well.

5 Try to organize other lawyers to work with the homeless. Lawyers may be more likely to respond to a request from one of their peers.

● **Contacts**
    Your local bar association
    The local Legal Aid office

YOU CAN
EMPLOY THE HOMELESS

As the saying goes, "It's hard to find good help these days." That's why some forward-thinking companies are recruiting employees from among the homeless. These companies have realized that supportive agencies can help them find many homeless people who are ready to work—and just need a break to get back on their feet.

Days Inn, the hotel chain, trains and employs homeless people for its reservation center in Atlanta, Georgia. It has employed more than forty homeless people in the last two years as reservation agents earning $4.80 to $5.90 an hour. Days Inn also provides homeless employees with hotel rooms for $5 per night and offers health insurance. Employees in this program are required to save a percentage of their salary toward a down payment on housing.

Sixty-six percent of those participating in the program stay on the job or move to a better one. Days Inn uses a screening procedure and accepts only candidates referred by shelters.

Carol Thompson, thirty-seven, the mother of a twelve-year-old son and two grown children, was a housekeeper in a hotel laundry in Atlanta, Georgia, when she became seriously ill two and a half years ago. Earning a salary barely over the minimum wage, Thompson had been just scraping by, so a week in the hospital and several weeks of recovery was enough to upset her financial situation. She lost her apartment. After staying with friends for a few weeks, Thompson and her son ended up in a shelter.

But five months later, Thompson's luck began to change. Days Inn contacted the shelter, looking for homeless people to train as reservationists. Thompson applied and was hired.

"I had never been on a computer before, ever in my life. I was real shaky about it. I really didn't think I had the ability to do it. But the Lord told me he was going to help me. He opened my mind. I could hear what they were saying. They really took patience with me to help me, and I passed. And I've been going hog wild ever since."

Thompson has been promoted and now earns $5.90 an hour arranging package vacation deals for tourists. She and her son have moved into a subsidized low-income apartment.

"We know the situation with the homeless is getting bad. The only way it's going to get better is if we all reach down and help them.

"When Days Inn first started this program, they had some sour lemons—people who were drunk or had the wrong attitude—but they didn't stop. They kept looking 'til they found people who would work out.

"Not all the homeless are drug addicts. A lot of times when people are devastated, they break. It takes them a while to get reestablished. When they decide to get over the trauma and get ready to start again, somebody has to be there to help them."

● What You Can Do

1 Make sure the personnel office of your employer or company contacts local homeless programs when they are hiring.

2 Help provide follow-up support to homeless employees.

3 Make sure your company realizes that homeless employees have a different set of problems from other employees and may need more time and understanding during their first days on the job.

● **Contact**

For advice on employing the homeless you can contact:

Days Inn of America, Inc.
2751 Buford Highway, NE
Atlanta, GA 30324
(404) 728-4451
Contact: Richard Smith

YOU CAN
OPEN DOORS TO THE MENTALLY ILL

Approximately 25 to 30 percent of the homeless population is mentally ill.
—National Alliance to End
Homelessness

Scarlet Wyant, forty-six, is a case manager at Horizon House in Philadelphia, where she supervises eighteen mentally ill people. She loves her job and does her best to help her clients. She's especially qualified for the job because she too has mental illness, which she keeps in check with medicine. What makes her credentials even more impressive, though, is that until three years ago, she was living on the street.

"I was on the street eight years. I was a student at Rutgers University, in political science. During my senior year I had a stress breakdown and lost my job and ended up on the streets. I had no money, nowhere to go. I lived on the streets [of Philadelphia] with the street people, eating out of garbage cans, surviving in that manner."

After eight years, Wyant's physical condition was deteriorating. Sister Mary Scullion, director of Women of Hope, a permanent residence for mentally ill women, got to know Wyant through her outreach program. Sister Mary would visit Wyant at her usual spot over a grate, and bring her food and talk with her. Finally, one cold winter day, when Wyant had become seriously ill, Sister Mary decided that for Wyant's own good, she had to be forcibly taken in.

"I was 302-ed, involuntary commitment to a hospital, and

placed in Woman of Hope. I stayed there two years while under psychiatric care. They gradually gave me little jobs, answering phones, cleaning up, minor stuff, until I graduated to bigger jobs. It's a long way back. When you're on the streets long enough, your mind doesn't function as well. You lose your actual physical skills. When they're bringing you back, it's like you're relearning life. You have to be taught how to shop, how to cook, how to dress. You're starting from zero. Your mind is blank. A lot of these people in shelters, they do nothing but stand around and sit because they don't know how to function. I had to have a nun go shopping with me. You don't know how to pick out your clothes, the simplest things.

"You go through a stage that you want to go back [to the streets]. You're facing responsibility. You're coming back into society. Out on the streets there are no rules or responsibilities. It's like living in a vacuum. You come and go as you please. There's no one to say that you have to do something.

"At Women of Hope, they start organizing you. You have to make your bed, take a shower, take care of yourself. That's the first step. The nun escorts you to a shower. And you have to take your medicine. Even though they can't legally force you to take medicine, they made sure I did. You don't tangle with the nuns.

"The people I worked with, especially the nuns and Sister Mary Scullion, had such faith in me that I could come back. They expressed that all the time, until I started working in Dignity Housing as a phone operator, and then worked with Project Share, and finally graduated to Horizon House, which is a tough job. It was their insistence that I could.

"I live with the constant fear of losing my job. I'm afraid to move into an apartment right now because I'm afraid I'll lose my job and it will start all over again. You get to a point where you're *afraid* that you'll go there [the streets] again. They say it will go away.

"A lot of homeless people don't expect life to improve. [They think] 'this is what my life is, this is what it will continue to be.' The streets and the homeless is not a subculture, it's a *culture.* They have their own social life. In the evenings the social life begins at ten o'clock. A lot of shelters have curfews. Once you put them in a shelter, you cut off their social life, and they go through a tremendous amount of isolation because they don't have their buddies and pals, which is what the system doesn't understand.

"Women of Hope doesn't have a curfew. I could come and go as I pleased.

"I would like people to understand one thing. There's a difference between homeless and the streets. They are different societies completely. Most of the homeless are in the shelters. A lot of the homeless work in McDonalds, in low-paying jobs. The streets are different people, most of them with addictions."

Since 1985 Women of Hope has helped more than 100 severely mentally ill women who had been living on the streets for long periods of time. All but a few have broken the cycle of homelessness. Many have moved on to independent living situations and employment, while others, like Wyant, live in supportive residences.

The Sisters of Mercy at Mercy Hospice operate the program, which is funded by the City of Philadelphia.

"People don't need a tremendous amount," remarks Sister Mary. "They just need the basics of housing, health care, employment, and education. And people who care. With that combination we have seen that the cycle of homelessness can be broken with tremendous success. There's no good reason why mentally disabled people should be forced to live on these streets."

● What You Can Do

Here are some ways you can help mentally ill homeless people:

⚡ Volunteer to work with an outreach program, bringing food, assistance, compassion, and conversation to mentally ill people on the street.

2 Donate money, clothes (such as coats, socks, thermal underwear), food or goods (such as umbrellas, sleeping bags, blankets) to outreach programs that assist the mentally ill homeless.

3 Volunteer at a mental health treatment center or permanent residence for the homeless, particularly if you are a trained counselor or social worker.

4 Beginning in the 1960s, the U.S. discharged thousands of mentally ill people from large mental institutions into the community. Smaller scale community facilities were supposed to be created to take them in, but these never materialized. That's why so many mentally ill people are homeless. Advocate for more community facilities for the mentally ill, including group homes.

5 Don't oppose group homes for the homeless mentally ill in your community. Rather, ask to be on their boards so that you can have a say in how they are run and the impact they make in the community.

6 When you see a homeless person who is mentally ill and about to harm himself or someone else, call 911. Try to keep the person in sight until help arrives. It may be better not to intervene unless it becomes critically necessary.

● **Contacts**

For information on how to help, you can contact:

National Institute of Mental Health
Office of Programs for the Homeless Mentally Ill
5600 Fishers Lane
Room 7C-06
Rockville, MD 20857
(301) 443-3706

National Resource Center on Homelessness and Mental Illness
Policy Research Associates, Inc.
262 Delaware Avenue
Delmar, NY 12054
(800) 444-7415

YOU CAN

ORGANIZE A FOOD OR CLOTHING DRIVE

We have the resources and knowledge to eliminate widespread hunger by the year 2000.

> —"Hunger Action Manual,"
> National Student Campaign
> Against Hunger

It's easy to organize a food or clothing drive because it's easy to find hungry people and people in need of clothing.

FOOD DRIVES

Contact your local shelter, soup kitchen, meal delivery program, or food pantry and arrange the dates of your food drive with them—when you will collect the food, and when you will drop it off to them. Ask the agency if there are any kinds of food they would especially like to receive, and what kinds of food they don't need.

There are several different ways to conduct a food drive. You can set up outside a supermarket on a weekend and ask people as they go in to purchase an item for your food drive. To do this you'll need:

Permission in advance from the store. (This is easier to obtain of you are part of an organized group like a church or synagogue.)

A large folding table to pile the food on.

A poster announcing to whom the food will be donated.

A leaflet to give out, outlining the services performed by the food program receiving the donated food.

Boxes or bags to carry the food away.

Transportation to deliver the food to its recipients.

Another way to collect food is to make an announcement about it at your church, synagogue, club, school, job, or other organization. Leave a large box in a busy area with a sign attached indicating that people can drop food donations in it, and who the donations are for.

In general, you will be collecting nonperishable foods— canned food (such as tuna, fruit, tomato sauce, beans, vegetables), rice, pasta, peanut butter, jam, powdered milk, sugar, honey, flour, coffee, tea, and the like.

Arrange to have a van or car available when the food is collected and ready to be taken to the delivery site.

The Columbia Jewish Congregation of Columbia, Maryland, conducts an ongoing food drive. A barrel is kept in the synagogue lobby, and Rabbi Martin Siegel regularly reminds the congregation to bring donations of food to put in it.

The food is distributed two ways. Some of it goes to a food pantry (a kind of food warehouse) that serves the poor of the whole county. The rest is given to neighborhood people who are in need.

"People come and tell us their situation and then they go and take what they want, like a grocery store," says Rabbi Siegel. "We don't stand over them and tell them what to take. We try to treat people with individuality and dignity—there are no forms or interviews. It's as simple and direct as possible.

"We're in an area that doesn't have large numbers of poor people. People in an area with more poor may have to do it with more restrictions."

CLOTHING DRIVES

Among the other social services that the synagogue provides is a clothing drive for local shelters.

"Twice a year we collect clothing to donate to shelters," Rabbi Siegel explains. "We do it simply and it works fine. We tell the congregation in advance, by announcing it at Friday night and Saturday morning services, to bring in clean clothes that they'd like to donate. We ask them to separate clothes between men and women, because they go to different shelters. We have a big truck parked in front of the building. People bring their stuff in bags. We give them receipts because the donations are tax deductible.

"We take everything. What the shelters can't use they can sell."

● What You Can Do

Some tips on mounting a food or clothing drive:

Find out what the need is. If area programs already have enough clothing, turn your attention elsewhere.

Find out what others are already doing. Don't duplicate efforts.

Decide on the best time. Winter and the holidays are a popular time for drives. Think about doing it in the spring or summer when need is great but supply meager.

Set modest goals. If you exceed them, you and your associates will feel happy with your efforts. But if your collection goals are so high that you don't meet them, people may feel let down and will be unlikely to go on to other projects.

● Contact

Columbia Jewish Congregation
5885 Robert Oliver Place
Columbia, MD 21045
(301) 730-6044
Contact: Rabbi Martin Siegel

YOU CAN

VOLUNTEER AT A SHELTER

New York City houses approximately 4,500 single adults in armory shelters every night.

Sometimes our efforts on behalf of these individual clients do not end the client's homelessness or solve all of his or her problems. Almost always, though, they provide respite to those wearied by endless experiences of being stepped around and over, rushed past, avoided, moved on, ridiculed and ignored.

—Legal Action Center for the Homeless

The atmosphere of homeless shelters varies, from small, cozy havens where guests get the best in social services, to huge congregate centers that house hundreds of people and offer minimal services. But the fundamental role of the volunteer is similar in all shelters. Wherever shelter volunteers work, they provide three basic types of service:

▸ Helping guests to get clean sheets, to obtain food and drink if available, and to follow sign-in procedures

▸ Offering human contact and companionship

▸ Suggesting where guests can go for services, and counseling them on how to claim benefits.

If you'd like to volunteer at a shelter, don't worry that you need particular skills or credentials to be a good worker. A willingness to help people is the main requirement.

Here are some tips that can help you be a more effective volunteer. In general, follow the rules of common courtesy, because it is as important to homeless people to be treated with respect as it is to anyone else.

—Introduce yourself and let the guest know you are a volunteer.

—Keep in mind that some guests are newcomers and others are regulars who know their way around. If possible, find out who the newcomers are and offer to orient them to the shelter.

—Offer assistance to anyone who has obvious pressing needs. If someone does not seem to want to talk, however, avoid putting him or her in the position of having to respond to you.

—Give guests time to get used to you. If a guest wants to be alone, then leave him or her in peace.

—When you do converse with a guest, try not to ask a lot of questions. Some guests have been questioned in so many welfare offices and clinics that they begin to interpret casual questions as an interrogation.

—Avoid talking about a guest in the third person, as if he or she wasn't there. This tends to happen if a volunteer is speaking on a guest's behalf, but it makes a person feel ignored.

—Make eye contact when you're talking to a guest, and try to give him or her your full attention.

One common mistake volunteers make is that they attempt to exert control over guests by nudging them to accept services they're unwilling or not ready to receive. Often, you can best help a guest by just *listening*. Try to adjust to each person's pattern of relating, and show him or her that you are concerned and supportive, just as you do in your social interactions outside the shelter.

David Suehsdorf, an actor and writer, has been a volunteer at the Men's Shelter at Riverside Church for five years. Located in New York City on the Upper West Side of Manhattan, this shelter is so comfortable and has such a nice atmosphere that it's known as the Waldorf of shelters.

The shelter houses ten men, all of whom have been screened by a local crisis center. This is not a facility where men can come in off the street; only men who are deemed likely to fit into the group are accepted.

"One of the reasons I joined Riverside Church was because of its social activism," says Suehsdorf. "I was interested in other areas, but I ended up one night volunteering at the shelter and after a hiatus I stayed with it.

"I do a lot of phone calling, getting volunteers, replacing volunteers. That is one of the least satisfying aspects of the work. But being there with the guys *is* satisfying. It just gives you a lot back."

The men can come in to the shelter at 7:30 P.M. when a volunteer opens the doors. Guests and volunteers make dinner together, and afterwards guests clean up. Then there's a social time, when the men play chess or backgammon or just talk. Lights out is at 11:00 P.M., when everybody goes to sleep or reads, guests in one room and the volunteers in an adjoining room. The alarm clock rings at 6:30 A.M. or so.

"Emotionally, it's very rewarding," says Suehsdorf. "The men's lives, their stories, their need to confide—without soliciting, nudging. You can sit down and share a cigarette and start talking about the Mets and . . . there are guys who are private, but most of them will get into the issues of their own lives and it's very compelling. These are life stories. That aspect is to me very enriching.

"You think you're going to get here and do your good work, but you find you get so much more back," Suehsdorf continues.

"There's a warmth—a kind of generosity at that level. You know there's a lot of games and manipulation, and there's a lot of foolishness. But these are guys who have hit bottom; there's a kind of resiliency and at times there can be a kind of cutting honesty.

"There are times I come home and I am so grateful for my wife and the roof over my head and the daughter who is crawling all over me at this moment. For warmth, for privacy."

What kinds of problems crop up for volunteers working with homeless men?

"There's an interesting phenomenon that I have noticed," Suehsdorf remarks. "The way I would put it is: Say a man is drowning in the river. You look round for something and you find a branch—and he won't take it. He says he wants a life preserver instead. And you don't have a life preserver. And I have seen a lot of times guys would rather go down than take the branch. You can stand there and say, 'Look, I wish I could give you a life preserver, but I don't have that. This is what we have.' And they won't take it. And we run into that more times than we'd wish. . . . This is the down side."

Still, Suehsdorf finds volunteering at the shelter gratifying. "Our program is highly regarded," he notes. "The shelter is comfortable, the guys eat well. When I say people like the shelter, I don't think I'm being prideful. This is not a bunch of diffident volunteers. The sense of commitment, the fellowship—the guys pick up on it. But sometimes it doesn't fit their agenda."

Suehsdorf explains, "A guy might ask for money, humble himself in that way; but he won't humble himself enough to walk through the threshold of the counseling service. That's a peculiar kind of pride."

Shelters provide only temporary housing and should not be considered an adequate response to the crisis of homelessness. The focus of all public and private efforts should be to *end* homelessness by getting people into decent, affordable, and permanent housing. Until that is accomplished, safe shelters provide a vital service.

• What You Can Do

1 Call your local homeless coalition or volunteer clearinghouse for information on shelters in your area. Then contact the shelter to volunteer.

2 If you are an inexperienced volunteer, you can look for a shelter that has some volunteer training. Local volunteer clearinghouses may also provide training.

3 If you're hesitant, try volunteering with a friend. You may feel more comfortable, and you'll have someone with whom to discuss the experience.

YOU CAN

LEND A HAND TO HOMELESS PEOPLE WITH AIDS

In New York City alone, it is conservatively estimated that there are at least 10,000 persons with HIV-related illness who are now without homes. Yet, some ten years into the epidemic, there are less than 250 units of supportive housing for people with AIDS in that city.
—National Coalition for the Homeless

The most useful thing you can volunteer to do is help them get housing. People with AIDS shouldn't be on the street.
—Penny Sarvis, San Francisco Network Ministries

People with AIDS often have a serious housing problem. Medical expenses coupled with intermittent employment may render them unable to afford housing. The lucky ones have friends and family to fall back on. The unlucky ones become homeless, shifting back and forth between hospitals and shelters—shelters that can hasten death because of increased exposure to opportunistic diseases.

Homeless people with AIDS need several types of housing corresponding to the cycle of their disease. These range from independent living arrangements to more service-intensive housing. There are several ways in which you can help.

● What You Can Do

1 Volunteer to work with homeless people with AIDS. People with AIDS have special emotional needs as well as housing needs. If you volunteer to work with people with AIDS, remember:

▶ Be willing to commit for a certain length of time—at least six months
▶ Be a good listener
▶ Be comfortable talking about feelings.

If you volunteer, you might choose one of several jobs:

▶ Provide legal assistance, if you're a lawyer
▶ Be a "buddy"
▶ Provide transportation to take people shopping or to medical appointments
▶ Help look for housing and provide follow-up assistance like doing chores and errands.

2 Act as an advocate for housing for people with AIDS. Support the creation of group homes and hospices. And don't oppose such housing when it is proposed for your neighborhood.

● **Contacts**
National AIDS Hotline
(800) 342-2437

National AIDS Information Clearinghouse
P.O. Box 6003
Rockville, MD 20850
(800) 458-5231

Or contact your local or state AIDS coalition.

YOU CAN

KNOW HOW TO RESPOND TO PANHANDLERS

The hungry need more than handouts. They need nurturing and support—they need involvement.
> —Marcia Ruth, Director of the
> Dinner Program for
> Homeless Women in
> Washington, DC

Because of their visibility and obtrusiveness, panhandlers have come to represent the entire homelessness crisis to many people. Seeing them, listening to their requests for a quarter or a dollar, we're reminded of poverty and of the grim reality of homelessness.

What should you do when a poor person asks you for a handout? "People have to follow their own consciences," advises Nan Roman, director of policy for the National Alliance to End Homelessness. "But remember, giving to people on the street is not the answer. It is not going to solve their problem. However, if you're genuinely concerned, look at the situation and make a decision based on that."

Roman elaborates: "Bear in mind that people who accost you for money are not always homeless. An alternative to giving them money is to contribute your funds to local programs that provide more permanent solutions."

● What You Can Do
TIPS FOR DEALING WITH PANHANDLERS

1 There's no one way to deal with panhandlers. You have to assess the situation and act accordingly. Is the person potentially dangerous? Does the person seem to be a "professional" hustler? Does the person seem really to need some money to get food?

2 Even if you're not going to give, a smile and a polite response are in order. But again, assess the situation and avoid opening yourself up to a confrontation.

3 In some areas service providers publish cards, fliers, or brochures telling people where to get help. If you want to respond to those you think need help, carry a few of these with you and give them out instead of change. Then give your money to one of the organizations listed on the brochure.

4 You can respond to a request for money with information. Say, "Do you know about the meal program down the street?" or "I support _____ transitional housing program. Do you know about their services?"

5 If you're being harassed by a panhandler, don't get into a confrontation. The hostility and aggression directed at you come from the panhandler's situation. Try to ignore the person or remove yourself from the situation.

Roman is also enthusiastic about the meal coupon system used by the Weingart Center in Los Angeles. Concerned people buy meal coupons for $2.50 each to give to panhandlers, who can exchange them for meals at the Weingart Center's cafeteria.

"The coupons provide people in need with a hot meal in a nice, clean environment," says Elizabeth Bailey, vice president of public relations for the Weingart Center. "It gives people some assurance that they're helping a person who is truly needy versus the person who is a hustler.

"When people give money to folks who are panhandling," Bailey continues, "you don't know if the person is going to use it for food or perhaps for drugs or alcohol. The coupon lets a person know it will indeed be used for food.

"Some corporations buy them in bulk and give them to their employees to pass out when they're at lunch," notes Bailey. "Others sell them in their company stores.

"The person who really wants a meal, they're thrilled. For

the person who wants to buy a bottle of whiskey, they're disappointed."

Bailey has this advice for shelters or other programs interested in setting up different kinds of coupon systems: "I would say to someone implementing this program, keep your mind open," Bailey asserts. "Try using the coupons for things other than food. They can be used for a night's shelter, or a bus token, or counseling."

● **Contact**

If you'd like to know more about the Weingart Center's meal coupon program, contact:

The Weingart Center
515 East 6th Street
Los Angeles, CA 90021
(213) 622-3629
Contact: Elizabeth Bailey
Vice President of Development and Public Relations

YOU CAN

GIVE SPECIAL HELP TO
BATTERED HOMELESS WOMEN

More than 58 percent of American women are battered by a husband or partner at some point in their lives. More than one third are battered repeatedly. Of men who batter their wives, 53 percent also abuse their children.

—National Coalition on
Domestic Violence

Homeless battered women are particularly vulnerable to the problems of life on the street. They have emerged from violent environments in which they have often been psychologically as well as physically abused. Sometimes they live in fear that their batterer will pursue them and hurt them again.

In practical terms, homeless battered women are often poorly educated and without income. They need comprehensive counseling and assistance to enable them to establish independent, violence-free households, especially if they have children.

Hotel Life
I live every day as best I can.
I have a great love for life.
In my life I've seen sorrow.
Through my children's eyes
I see the future like a rocket to the moon.
I see hope, I see so much good and beauty
Like a glowing light right in the middle of my room.
When I think I'll never get out of here,
I see happiness for me,

I see another world, a better world.
I have learned to laugh through these eyes.
And cry.
—Gloria McDaniels, a formerly homeless woman
(This poem was written as part of a therapeutic workshop for homeless women receiving services from the Jewish Board of Family and Children's Services.)

Mary Robertson, executive director of the Center for Battered Women in Austin, Texas, is tired of people who act naïve when discussing what can be done to help homeless battered women.

"It's no mystery. What we need is money," Robertson asserts. "You can vote for enough tax money to support the organizations that have the expertise to help these people. There are programs and agencies ready to help. It's a problem of resources, of not enough low-income housing, not enough job-training programs that provide day care—that's a big thing for our women. There are not enough programs to help with the first month's rent or deposits on utilities."

The Center for Battered Women, which opened in 1977, gives shelter to over a thousand women and children a year. Thousands more receive counseling and support services, and the Center runs a twenty-four-hour crisis hotline, operated by volunteers.

"I'm sure there can't be a nicer shelter facility in the whole country," says Robertson.

The Center has room to shelter forty-five women and children, and it's always full. It can serve only 27 percent of the women who apply for shelter.

The main function of the volunteers who work at the Center is to handle the hotline. Volunteers go through training to learn how to handle crisis calls. They also help with housekeeping tasks.

"A big issue for us is transportation," Robertson notes. "We need more volunteers who can be on call to transport women to appointments and pick women up in the middle of the night if they need to leave home."

Robertson hopes to expand the Center's services. "After the women leave the shelter, we'd like to have a program where we have a follow-up case worker. Part of that would be to help the woman in her situation as a single parent and to provide moral support to her. Volunteers could help with parenting issues."

Many of the women need legal assistance. "The biggest resource we don't have is lawyers to do pro bono work to help these women. Even if technically the women have assets, they typically don't have access to them." This means that a woman may be co-owner—with her husband—of the house she has fled, or a car, or she may own stocks or have valuables in a bank deposit box. But if she has left her husband, he may prevent her from selling her property until she returns to him or until the court releases her assets. This could take months or even years.

Because batterers, as men, generally earn more money than the women they batter, says Robertson, "The batterers usually have more resources for legal help, so the women get outclassed in their legal representation. This affects property settlements, custody disputes, a lot of other matters."

● **Contact**

If you'd like to volunteer at a shelter for battered women, or become an advocate for legislation to support funds and programs for battered homeless women, call or write to:

The National Coalition Against Domestic Violence
P.O. Box 34103
Washington, DC 20043-4103
(202) 638-6388

Or contact your local United Way or social service agency.

Gail Rice is the coordinator of volunteers for the Austin Center for Battered Women. She has worked with thousands of battered women and their children. Here is the story of one family she helped.

"Barbara was admitted to the shelter with two little boys. She had been badly beaten repeatedly over a period of several years. She had left her husband a couple of times and gone back, but she left for good when he picked up one of her sons and shook him so violently the boy got a detached retina and was permanently blinded in that eye.

"She had no job, no source of income, two very troubled children, literally no resources. She herself was legally blind and needed corrective treatment. Her mother had recently died. She was in a terrible way.

"But she was at the point of being determined to change her life. She had reached that point, that women do reach, of realizing that there is no going back and making a life with their violent partner.

"So she made very good use of the counseling and support we were able to give her. When she left the Center, she was able to get a low-paying job. Eventually she went to a junior college for two years and got a paramedic degree.

"She has even started an activist group to work for better enforcement of child support laws in the state of Texas.

"After she got out of the bad relationship, she was on her own for four or five years, so she built back her own identity and got very clear on who she was. She is remarried now.

"Both her boys needed a lot of counseling to help their emotional scars heal. . . . They're doing well in school.

"For a lot of women like Barbara, to be able to build back their life, they have to have incredible grit, the kind of grit to work two jobs. There was no safety net for her. She had to put her own safety net together stitch by stitch."

It was clear that the woman was ready to take the necessary steps to free herself from abuse. "You saw that she had no self-esteem and she had an incredible list of problems, but she had the spirit. That was very visible. You could see she was capable and that with support she was going to make it.

"Battered women need somebody in their corner, some attention, someone saying, 'You can do it. You're not alone, we're here.' Volunteers are a source of this kind of support and connection.

"She came back and worked as a volunteer at the Center. Helped on the hotline and with emergency transportation and helped train volunteers. She gave a lot back to the Center and to other battered women.

"It makes me happy and it's a thrill to have had a small part in that."

People who volunteer at shelters for battered women provide an essential service.

"I would say that while their contribution in terms of time and energy may seem small, it may provide a vital piece in the solution. By providing support at the right time, the individual can make a terrific difference.

"We very much depend on volunteers, in two ways. By coming into the shelters and outreach centers and doing the work. And going back into the communities with raised consciousness and awareness and talking to their friends and other women and recruiting other people into the work."

YOU CAN
RAISE FUNDS TO HELP THE HOMELESS

In 70 percent of the survey cities, shelters must turn away homeless families because of lack of resoures.
—"A Status Report on Hunger and Homelessness in America's Cities: 1990," The United States Conference of Mayors

If you would like to provide monetary support to help the homeless, look to organizations that are finding *long term* ways to end the problem.

"Think permanent solutions," suggests Susan Baker, chairman of the Alliance. "Think how your financial contribution can *end* the problem rather than contain it. Of course, emergency programs are necessary and worthy, but we need to consider how our dollars and our expertise can be used to find long-term solutions to homelessness.

"Give money to organizations that are actively working to move people from shelters to permanent housing. Support organizations that are increasing the supply of affordable housing for people who have been homeless."

Some practical ways to funnel money to homelessness organizations include:

Encourage your company to start a matching gift program (if it doesn't already have one) so that every dollar you give will be matched by your company.

Find a volunteer activity that will help raise money. See if your company would be interested in assisting that project, and encourage your co-workers, neighbors, or church to co-sponsor an event or make a financial contribution.

Some tried and true ways to make money include:

▶ Craft sales
▶ Bake sales
▶ Book sales
▶ Golf benefits
▶ Auctions of merchandise donated by individuals as well as stores and companies
▶ Raffles
▶ Benefit parties to which guests can bring a contribution or buy tickets.

However you raise money, determine in advance to which homeless organization the proceeds will go, and provide leaflets about the organization to participants and contributors to your fund-raising project, so they can be informed about the organization's services.

● **What You Can Do**

1 Get involved in your company's philanthropic program, if possible. Encourage its support of projects to help the homeless.

2 If you're a good writer or researcher, or have development experience, see if a local homeless assistance organization needs help preparing funding proposals. Fund-raising is often a time-consuming task that draws an organization's staff resources away from direct service to the homeless.

For information about worthy national organizations that help homeless people, see the list at the end of this book.

A valuable resource book with ideas for fund-raising events, lists of foundations, and other information is: *Creative Sources of Funding for Programs for Homeless Families,* by Dorothy Siemon (Washington, DC: Georgetown University Child Development Center).

The book is available for $7 from:
Georgetown University Child Development Center
3800 Reservoir Road, NW
Washington, DC 20007
(202) 687-8635

YOU CAN

VOLUNTEER AT A SOUP KITCHEN

The body is like a furnace, and food is the energy that keeps it going. When there's not enough energy, the body slows down, conserving the little fuel it does have. So if some homeless people seem lethargic, apathetic, not much interested in getting up and going, I would bet that is more reflective of their diet than their attitude.
> —Dr. Audrey Cross, Columbia University School of Public Health

Forty-two percent of people eating in soup kitchens eat one meal or less per day.
> —Legal Action Center for the Homeless

Feeding the hungry is the most fundamental service society can provide. It's also one of the most rewarding because whenever people get together to eat, they feel better afterwards.

Soup kitchens depend on volunteers. Whether you go in as an individual or volunteer as a group to take responsibility for a whole meal, your local soup kitchen will be happy to accept your help.

Arnold Jones, a retired IBM executive, volunteers at a soup kitchen in an Episcopal church near his home in Raleigh, North Carolina. He enjoys the work and finds it very rewarding.

"I've been volunteering in the soup kitchen once a week, for a year," estimates Jones. "My Sunday school class decided we should take on some socially oriented project to help people in need. So every Friday we supply some two to six people to work in the soup kitchen. It's a demonstration of our Christian love, you could say."

Jones describes the work he does on a typical morning at the soup kitchen. "We start at nine A.M. and we prepare food for two hours. We don't organize anything. The day captain tells us what to do. But by now we don't even have to be told. We'll make up some lemonade. That's easy. Or we'll put out doughnuts on trays. We'll make sandwiches. And we prepare different dishes from the food that is donated."

Initially surprised by the quality of food served at the soup kitchen, Jones now takes pride in serving good meals to the needy. "Some generous supermarkets give us day-old baked goods. Companies give us cafeteria food that they haven't used. Some of it is really good. We get food from some of the best restaurants in town: flounder stuffed with crabmeat, prime rib.

"We make the food for two hours and we serve it from eleven to twelve," Jones goes on to explain. "We're able to serve 100 to 225 people in an hour, cafeteria style. We hand them the food, even the cakes and danish, because we want to have interaction between the volunteers and the folks who come in there. We very definitely try to be cheerful and give them an encouraging word.

"We let the people go through the line as many times as they wish. It's all you can eat. But there are certain things we have to limit because they'll take a lot of them, like meat sandwiches."

Jones summed up the soup kitchen's philosophy this way: "Keep it simple. Keep it structured." That approach, he says, seems to work well.

"You get all types of reactions from the patrons," Jones says. "Some of them are courteous and some of them are mean and sullen. But for the most part—and this is sort of tragic—many of them seem to have almost retired from human intercourse. Their face is a blank, they don't say thank you, they seem to be just existing."

Who volunteers at the soup kitchen? "A lot of the workers

are women; some of them are from the Junior League. And sometimes we get young people who work because they like to do something worthwhile. When we have teenagers working, that really adds a lot. The patrons like the kids. We had two little girls working one week, I think they were eleven or twelve, and the patrons were seemingly more gracious. The kids cheer up the place.

"We clean up between twelve and one," Jones concludes. "I wipe down tables, fold up chairs and put them up, wash the big pots and pans. Whatever food is left we take over to the rescue mission and the Salvation Army. They feed people at night. We recycle the food."

Jones heartily recommends volunteering at a soup kitchen to those looking for a way to help the homeless. "Most people would derive satisfaction from doing this if they would try it on for size. When I conclude my four hours there, I feel very satisfied."

● **What You Can Do**

1 Contact a soup kitchen at a church or shelter near you, and ask if they need volunteers. You can locate soup kitchens through local charitable organizations, like the Salvation Army.

2 See if there's a mobile feeding program in your area. In mobile programs, vans deliver sandwiches and other food to people on the street. Volunteer to make food, to drive, or to distribute food. Or get together a group of people to take food out to the homeless, under the auspices of a service organization.

3 Make food and deliver it to a soup kitchen. Be sure to find out what they need first.

4 Many soup kitchens rely on donated food. Volunteer to pick up donations from stores, caterers, etc.

5 Have your organization or congregation assume responsibility for providing and serving food one day each month (or week, or year) at a local program for the homeless. This might mean buying, fixing, and serving the food.

YOU CAN

GET INVOLVED IN HOME SHARING

Thirty-eight percent of homeless people were evicted from their homes within the past year.
—U.S. Department of Housing
and Urban Development

One of the innovative ways people have found to deal with the housing shortage is to work out home-sharing arrangements. Under such programs, people who have space in their homes offer it to those who seek housing in exchange for rent or for help around the house. This is a mutually beneficial system; not only does it increase the options of those looking for housing, it allows those who already have a home to get extra income or free household help. It may help them reduce expenses, hold on to their home, and prevent them from becoming homeless themselves.

Obviously, working out living arrangements between strangers can be complicated, and this kind of program requires sensitive management and counseling to succeed.

The Red Cross conducts a home-sharing program in Manassas, Virginia. Here are the groups of people it works well for:

1. Those who need some supplemental income in order to keep their house or apartment.

2. People in need of short-term housing because they're on a waiting list for public housing or are newly arrived in the area.

3. People who are newly separated, divorced, or widowed.

4. Single parents who need help with child care or who can't afford decent housing on one income.

5. Young working people who require roommates in order to afford to live in an area.

6. Elderly people who need supplemental income, companionship, or household help.

7. Handicapped people who require live-in help to stay in their own homes.

8. People who can only afford adequate housing by doing household help for the home-provider.

The Red Cross home-sharing program is available to people of all ages, ethnic groups, and socioeconomic levels. However, the Red Cross has found that this type of program is not for everyone, and they don't promise to find housing for everyone. The program tends *not* to be successful for the following groups of people:

1. Parents with two or more children.

2. Alcoholics or substance abusers who are not in recovery.

3. People with a history of violent behavior.

4. People for whom a halfway house or other treatment facility would be more suitable.

5. Those who are unwilling to pay their way with money or services.

● What You Can Do

1 If you would like to develop a home-sharing program under the auspices of your club, temple, church, or other organization, here are some guidelines suggested by the Red Cross program:

▶ Require all applicants—both those with homes and those seeking housing—to come in for a personal interview in the office.

▶ Have them bring with them three recent references.

▶ Make sure you *check* all references.

▶ Interview potential home-providers *in their homes.*

▶ Insist that all applicants sign a disclaimer form, freeing you and your group from liability.

HOMESEEKER FORM
Red Cross, Prince William Chapter

Applicant Number: _____

Date: _____
Referral: _____
Interviewer: _____
Social Security: _____

Client

Name: _____
Address: _____
_____
Phone: _____
Living With: _____ How Long: _____
Family Living in Area: _____ Phone: _____
Marital Status: S M D W SEP. How Long: _____
Hobbies, Interests: _____
_____

Age: _____
Race: _____
Religion: _____
Languages: _____
Dependents: _____
Health: _____
Medication: _____
Smokes: _____ Drinks: _____
Pets: _____ Drugs: _____

Work

Name: _____
Address: _____
Position: _____ How Long: _____
Work Background: _____

Phone: _____
Hours: _____
Drives: _____ Has Car: _____
Date/Apply: _____

Preferences & Requirements

Area(s): _____
Sex: _____ Parent With Child: _____ Age Range: _____
Smoking: _____ Drinking: _____ Overnight Guests: _____ Group Living: _____
Furniture: _____ Kitchen Priv.: _____ Stairs: _____
Transportation: _____ Pets: _____
Other: _____ Urgency: _____

Ability to Pay

Rent: _____ Income: _____ Sources: _____

Services

_____

References

_____
_____
_____

Phone: _____
Phone: _____
Phone: _____

Observations

_____

▶ Develop a form for all applicants to fill out. On the next page is the homeseeker form used by the Home Sharing Program of the Prince William, Virginia, chapter of the Red Cross. A similar, but not identical form can be developed for home providers.

2 Think about your own situation. If you would like to share your house with a homeless person, contact a local home-share program, or shelter or transitional housing program. Or call the United Way to find out who can help you. Be sure that, if you take in someone who is homeless, the service agency will provide follow-up support.

● **Contact**

If you would like further information about home-sharing programs, contact:

Red Cross, Prince William Chapter
9317 West Street
Manassas, VA 22110
(703) 368-4511
Contact: Lyn Costello, Chapter Manager

YOU CAN

RESTORE LIFE'S SIMPLE PLEASURES TO THE HOMELESS

Perhaps the clearest impact wrought by gathering despair among many of the homeless is our survey finding that the numbers of chronic or "hard-core" homeless have grown in the vast majority of participating cities and localities. These are mostly single adults who have simply given up seeking the help they need from our existing assistance system, because they feel the "system" has given up on them and is largely unresponsive to their needs . . .

—Moving Forward
The Partnership for the
Homeless

What we often forget when we see a homeless person is that not only do their bodies lack care and sustenance, but they miss the comfort of conversation, books, music, and peaceful reflection that we take for granted.

"It's the simple things in life—having conversations with friends, being complimented when you've done something well, hearing music or seeing beautiful things—that can give you the reinforcement you need," according to Susan Baker, chairman of the National Alliance to End Homelessness. "We shouldn't neglect this side of life when we think about what we can do to help homeless people."

● **What You Can Do**

1 Volunteer to bring musical performances, books, or other enrichment programs to people living in transitional housing.

2 Organize a theater, writing, or painting program for homeless people.

3 In a transitional housing program you can organize outdoor sports or exercise events.

4 Take children living in shelters on field trips to the circus, museums, the movies, the ballet, ice skating, bowling, swimming, and to special events like parades and fireworks.

YOU CAN
START A FOOD RECYCLING
PROGRAM

*It is estimated that Americans waste more than 200
billion pounds of food every year—approximately 20
percent of our total food production.*
> —National Student Campaign
> Against Hunger and
> Homelessness

Ever wonder what happens to all the trays of food on display in the cafeteria at your job? What do restaurants do with their extra bread and rolls at the end of the night? It can't all be turned into bread crumbs. What about all those unsold pies and cakes at supermarkets and doughnut shops?

Well, the bad news is that a lot of it goes to waste. But the good news is that more and more people are thinking creatively and recycling their excess food by donating it to transitional housing programs and soup kitchens, and to social service agencies that can distribute it to the poor.

City Harvest began in 1982 in New York City, when volunteers using a borrowed van started collecting food from restaurants, corporate dining rooms, and businesses and distributed it to the poor. Today City Harvest has five vans, which its employees use almost around the clock to collect food from about 3,000 sources. They distribute it to nearly 100 shelters, soup kitchens, church pantries, senior citizen and day-care centers—at a cost of only thirty-nine cents a meal.

Domenick Perciballi, delivery supervisor for City Harvest, is proud of what the organization accomplishes for the needy every day.

"We moved 277,000 pounds of food this month," he says in his busy office. "We operate this way: Say a donor calls and says they have a trailer load of potatoes—50,000 pounds of potatoes—usually out of Maine. I'll arrange for them to make a delivery to an agency that needs potatoes. Then I coordinate with other agencies that have trucks and are looking for food. We'll all meet at the delivery site to distribute the potatoes, and that cuts down on my expenses.

"All of the agencies are really cooperative in picking up food for themselves," Perciballi remarks. "And of course, we use our vans to deliver to agencies that don't have their own transportation."

City Harvest even tries to fill any special requests shelters or soup kitchens might have.

"Sometimes we'll get a phone call that some program is having a party for the children or a barbecue," Perciballi explains. "We try to fill the need, if we can. Maybe a studio that's been shooting a commercial will call and say, 'We've got 200 gallons of ice cream for you,' and we'll pick it up and deliver it to agencies."

Perciballi offers the following tips for people who want to set up a food recycling network like City Harvest:

"You would have to go to the local government and find out what the laws are for dealing with food. Donors are very skeptical about being sued for bad food. But a Good Samaritan law can cover that. And you can tell donors that their gifts are tax exempt.

"Then you get a good board of directors who are concerned and can raise money."

● What You Can Do

1 If there is a food recycling network in your community, it may need volunteers to transport food to the needy. If there isn't such a program, you may be able to start one. Contact Second Harvest (see address at the end of this chapter), a national network of 183 food banks that provide food to service agencies such as church pantries, soup kitchens, and youth centers that serve food. If you want to set up a neighborhood recycling program, Second Harvest can refer you to an agency.

2 Another possibility is to start or assist a local gleaning program, which involves letting poor people obtain surplus produce directly from area farms. Simply ask farmers if you can go into their fields after they have harvested, to pick up produce that has been overlooked or which has been left behind because of slight imperfections. Gleaning operations can either provide food to charities and churches, who in turn distribute to needy people, or gleaners can distribute the produce directly to needy people—or even arrange for them to go into the fields themselves to glean.

If you're working with a nonprofit charity, the value of the gleaned produce may be tax deductible to the farmer, providing an added incentive to his participation. Be prepared to provide him or her with a receipt.

● **Contacts**

For information about setting up a food recycling program in your community:

Second Harvest National Headquarters
343 South Dearborn
Suite 408
Chicago, IL 60604
(312) 263-2303

For information about setting up a gleaning program:

Senior Gleaners, Inc.
3185 Longview
North Highlands, CA 95660
Contact: Lonnie Beard
(916) 971-1530

LIST OF MAJOR ORGANIZATIONS
THAT HELP THE HOMELESS

The American Institute of Architects developed The Search for Shelter, a project which promotes the local development of housing for the homeless. Contact:

The American Institute of Architects
1735 New York Avenue, NW
Washington, DC 20006
(202) 626-7300

Over 500 Red Cross chapters provide services to the homeless. These include eviction prevention assistance, food, housing vouchers, shelter, and more. Contact:

American Red Cross
National Headquarters
17th and D Streets, NW
Washington, DC 20006
(202) 639-3610

The Better Homes Foundation funds programs to provide or improve a continuum of services to homeless families. Contact:

Better Homes Foundation
189 Wells Avenue
Newton Center, MA 02159
(617) 964-3834

Catholic Charities, USA, is the official service arm of the Catholic Church. Homeless programs funded by Catholic Charities include emergency shelters, transitional housing programs, SROs, and a range of other services. Contact:

Catholic Charities, USA
1319 F Street, NW
Washington, DC 20004
(202) 639-8400

The Center on Budget and Policy Priorities analyzes and reports on the national debate over government policies dealing with the needs of low- and moderate-income Americans. Contact:

Center on Budget and Policy Priorities
236 Massachusetts Ave., NE
Suite 305
Washington, DC 20002
(202) 544-0591

The Council of Jewish Federations represents Jewish social service organizations across the country. Contact:

Council of Jewish Federations
227 Massachusetts Ave., NW
Washington, DC 20002
(202) 547-0020

Created by Congress in 1983, the Emergency Food and Shelter Program funds local emergency food and shelter efforts throughout the country. Six major charitable organizations and a federal government representative sit on a National Board and oversee the distribution of funds to localities, based on poverty and unemployment statistics. Contact:

Emergency Food and Shelter
National Board Program
601 N. Fairfax Street
Suite 225
Alexandria, VA 22314-2088
(703) 683-1166

The Enterprise Foundation, through a national network of neighborhood and community organizations, helps the poor obtain housing and jobs. The Foundation provides technical assistance and low-interest loans. Contact:

Enterprise Foundation
505 American City Building
Columbia, MD 21044
(301) 964-1230

Habitat for Humanity is an international organization that builds and renovates housing for low-income people. Contact:

Habitat for Humanity
Habitat and Church Streets
Americus, GA 31709
(912) 924-6935

HandsNet is a national communications network that gathers and disseminates information and resources among organizations working to combat hunger, homelessness, and poverty. Contact:

HandsNet, Inc.
303 Potrero Street
Suite 54
Santa Cruz, CA 95060
(408) 427-0527

The Homelessness Information Exchange is a national service that collects, summarizes, and disseminates information on programs and policies concerning homelessness. Contact:

Homelessness Information Exchange
1830 Connecticut Ave., NW
Washington, DC 20009
(202) 462-7551

The Housing Assistance Council is a national nonprofit corporation dedicated to increasing the availability of decent housing for rural low-income people. Contact:

Housing Assistance Council
1025 Vermont Avenue, NW
Suite 606
Washington, DC 20005
(202) 842-8600

Established by Congress in 1987 as part of the Stewart B. McKinney Homeless Assistance Act, the Interagency Council monitors and evaluates federal homeless activities, collects and disseminates information, and studies problems related to homelessness. Contact:

Interagency Council on the Homeless
451 7th Street, SW
Washington, DC 20410
(202) 708-1480

Founded by the Ford Foundation in 1979, LISC channels private-sector financial resources to nonprofit community development corporations. Contact:

Local Initiatives Support Corporation
666 Third Avenue
New York, NY 10017
(212) 949-8560

Mental Health Law Project is a national nonprofit organization that advocates for people with mental disabilities who rely on the public sector for the services. MHLP's nationwide program, Community Watch, offers technical assistance to help housing providers and advocates overcome legal barriers to the development of community-living arrangements for children and adults with mental disabilities. Contact:

Mental Health Law Project
2021 L Street, NW
Suite 800
Washington, DC 20036-4909
(202) 467-5730

The National Alliance to End Homelessness is a national, nonprofit organization whose mission is to address the long-term problems of homelessness. The Alliance accomplishes its mission by bringing together all sectors of society in a program of research, advocacy, project operation, and education. It publishes a monthly newsletter, "Alliance," which contains information on resources, legislation, publications, upcoming conferences, etc. Contact:

National Alliance to End Homelessness
1518 K Street, NW
Suite 206
Washington, DC 20005
(202) 638-1526

NACHC is a nonprofit membership association and public policy advocacy organization representing community and migrant health centers, Health Care for the Homeless projects funded under the Stewart B. McKinney Act, black-lung clinics, and other health provider organizations that promote quality primary health care for the indigent and underserved. Contact:

National Association of Community Health Centers
1330 New Hampshire Avenue, NW

Suite 122
Washington, DC 20036
(202) 659-8008

NASW is a membership organization of social workers, many of whom provide services to the homeless. The organization coordinates a number of programs aimed at serving the homeless. Contact:

National Association of Social Workers
7981 Eastern Avenue
Silver Spring, MD 20910
(301) 565-0333

National Coalition for the Homeless is a national advocacy organization committed to decent and humane shelter and permanent housing for the homeless. Contact:

National Coalition for the Homeless
1439 Rhode Island Ave., NW
Washington, DC 20005
(202) 659-3310
or
105 East 22nd Street
New York, NY 10010
(212) 460-8110

The National Council of Churches is an ecumenical organization that brings together Protestant and Orthodox denominations as a deliberative body. Contact:

National Council of Churches of Christ in the USA
110 Maryland Avenue, NE
Washington, DC 20002
(202) 544-2350

The National Governors' Association monitors legislation concerning housing and homelessness in general and the implementation of McKinney Act programs in particular. Contact:

National Governors' Association
Hall of the States
444 North Capitol Street
Suite 250
Washington, DC 20001
(202) 624-7819

The Office of Programs for the Homeless Mentally Ill coordinates research, service demonstration, and technical assistance efforts for the homeless mentally ill population. Contact:

National Institute of Mental Health
Office of Programs for the Homeless Mentally Ill
5600 Fishers Lane
Room 7C-06
Rockville, MD 20857
(301) 443-3706

The National Low Income Housing Coalition is an organization of low-income housing advocates and organizations that supports improved low-income housing policies. Its educational arm, the Low Income Housing Information Service (LIHIS), publishes a monthly newsletter, "The Low Income Housing Round-Up," that follows related legislation. Contact:

National Low Income Housing Coalition
1012 14th Street, NW
Suite 1006
Washington, DC 20005
(202) 662-1530

The National Resource Center, under contract to the National Institute of Mental Health, provides technical assistance and comprehensive information concerning the needs of homeless mentally ill persons. Contact:

National Resource Center on Homelessness and Mental Illness
Policy Research Associates, Inc.
262 Delaware Avenue
Delmar, NY 12054
(800) 444-7415

The Neighborhood Reinvestment Corporation is a public, nonprofit corporation whose purpose is to revitalize declining lower-income neighborhoods for the benefit of current residents and to provide affordable housing. Contact:

Neighborhood Reinvestment Corporation
1325 G Street, NW
Suite 800
Washington, DC 20005
(202) 376-2400

The Salvation Army is an international religious and charitable organization dedicated to meeting the physical, spiritual, and emotional needs of people. The Salvation Army is one of the major providers of assistance to the homeless in the nation, operating hundreds of local shelters and comprehensive service programs. Contact:

Salvation Army
799 Bloomfield Avenue
Verona, NJ 07044
(201) 239-0606

Second Harvest is a nonprofit network of more than 200 food banks that secures donations of food and grocery items from the food industry. It then passes these donated goods via food banks to some 39,000 charitable agencies serving the needy and homeless. Begun in 1979, the Second Harvest network now distributes well over a million pounds of food a day. Agencies receive products for free, but they support their local food bank by paying a shared maintenance fee. Second Harvest has capped these fees at twelve cents per pound. To locate the Second Harvest food bank serving your area, contact:

Second Harvest Western Regional Office
5121 Port Chicago Highway
Concord, CA 94520
(415) 682-4555

Second Harvest Central Region Office
343 South Dearborn
Suite 408
Chicago, IL 60604
(312) 341-0581

Second Harvest Eastern Region Office
4 East Biddle Street
Baltimore, MD 21202
(301) 539-4944

Travelers Aid International is a network of local agencies that provides information and assistance to thousands of travelers, homeless people, runaway youth, etc. TAI agencies provide shelter, transitional housing programs, counseling, and other services. Contact:

Travelers Aid International
1001 Connecticut Ave., NW
Suite 504
Washington, DC 20036
(202) 659-9468

The U.S. Conference of Mayors' Task Force on Hunger and Homelessness has produced numerous reports on the status of housing, poverty, hunger, and homelessness in many major cities throughout the country. Contact:

U.S. Conference of Mayors
1620 Eye Street, NW
Washington, DC 20006
(202) 293-7330

United Ways are the largest funders of programs (soup kitchens, shelters, food banks, substance abuse, and emergency services) dealing with hunger and homelessness. Contact:

United Way of America
701 North Fairfax Street
Alexandria, VA 22314-2045
(703) 836-7100

World SHARE is a community-based, not-for-profit corporation that provides a monthly supplemental food package to those willing to help themselves and others.

SHARE-USA is a network of independently incorporated SHARE programs operating in the U.S. with the common goal of using self-help methods to end hunger in America. SHARE-USA coordinates network activities and provides centralized purchasing, training, and consulting to the local programs. Centralized purchasing offers volume foodbuying discounts. By networking, SHARE programs across the country are maximizing strengths, pooling resources, and bringing a better food value for the dollar to the families participating at each location.
Contact:

World Share
5255 Lovelock Street
San Diego, CA 92110
(619) 294-2981

BIBLIOGRAPHY

Checklist for Success: Programs to Help the Hungry and Homeless. Washington, DC: Prepared for the Emergency Food and Shelter National Board Program by the National Alliance to End Homelessness, 1990.

Helping the Homeless in Your Community. Washington, DC: Homelessness Information Exchange, 1989.

Housing and Homelessness: A Report of the National Alliance to End Homelessness. Washington, DC: The National Alliance to End Homelessness, 1988.

Kozol, Jonathan, *Rachel and Her Children: Homeless Families in America.* New York: Crown, 1988.

Lives in the Balance: Establishing Programs for the Homeless. Columbus, OH: The Ohio Coalition for the Homeless, 1988.

Porter, Kathryn H. *Poverty in Rural America: A National Overview.* Washington, DC: Center on Budget and Policy Priorities, 1989.

Responding to the Needs of the Homeless and Hungry. Washington, DC: American Red Cross, 1989.

Schorr, Lisbeth B., with Daniel Schorr. *Within Our Reach.* New York: Doubleday, 1988.

What Corporations Can Do to End Homelessness. Washington, DC: The National Alliance to End Homelessness, 1990.

Working With Homeless People. New York: Columbia University Community Services, 1988.

ABOUT THE NATIONAL ALLIANCE
TO END HOMELESSNESS

The National Alliance to End Homelessness is one of the oldest and largest national organization dedicated to fighting homelessness. Founded in 1983, the Alliance is recognized as the leading authority on homelessness in America.

The group gives technical assistance to service providers, conducts research, holds conferences on homelessness, and serves as an advocate for the homeless on Capitol Hill with federal agencies and in the private sector. The Alliance works with corporations and local governments nationwide to develop programs targeted at preventing homelessness. It works to provide skills and resources to organizations on the front line of the struggle to end homelessness.

Help fight homelessness, become a member of The National Alliance to End Homelessness. For information please call: (202) 638-1526.